JOE ALVES

DESIGNING
JAWS

JOE ALVES
DESIGNING JAWS

ISBN: 9781789091014

Published by Titan Books
A division of Titan Publishing Group Ltd.
144 Southwark St.
London
SE1 0UP

First edition: NOVEMBER 2019
1 3 5 7 9 10 8 6 4 2

Did you enjoy this book? We love to hear from our readers.
Please e-mail us at: readerfeedback@titanemail.com or write to Reader
Feedback at the above address.

To receive advance information, news, competitions, and exclusive offers online,
please sign up for the Titan newsletter on our website: www.titanbooks.com

A CIP catalogue record for this title is available from the British Library.

Printed and bound in China.

Our thanks and appreciation for additional photos and contributions from these fine folks:

Cal Acord, Jim Beller, Charlie Blair, Edith Blake, Denise Bratton, Andy Caulfield,
Carol Fligor, Ritchie Helmer, Douglas Kennedy, Chris Kiszka, Wayne Lacono, Jan Lauridsen,
Jerri Lauridsen, Susan Murphy, Greg Nicotero, Matt Taylor, Clint Schultz, Rita Orr-Schmidt,
Cory Turner (NPR), Dick Whitney, Al Wilde

Special thanks to Universal Archives and Amblin Partners for use of additional stills,
artwork, and the JAWS logo.

JOE ALVES

DESIGNING JAWS

WRITTEN BY DENNIS L. PRINCE   FOREWORD BY GREG NICOTERO

TITAN BOOKS

CONTENTS

FOREWORD
BY GREG NICOTERO

IN THIS DAY AND AGE, when knowledge and information are literally at your fingertips, there is a notion that, in some instances, we have learned all we can on certain subjects. In the not-so-distant past, effort and energy were required to gather information; today it all comes to us with the flick of a few fingers. For movie-going fans and filmmakers, this couldn't be more true today.

As a young and voracious film fan eager for anything and everything related to movies – and, more specifically, the "how'd they do that?" sentiment the movie-going experience provided – I dug deep into the background of the films that inspired me. One such film changed the direction of modern cinema in countless ways and continues to do so today. Its admirers have dissected the script, the behind-the-scenes stories and its players repeatedly for the past four decades… and that film is JAWS.

I was one of those fans who pored over Carl Gottlieb's The JAWS Log, Edith Blake's The Making of the Movie JAWS and, most recently, Matt Taylor's encyclopedic JAWS: Memories from Martha's Vineyard. My perpetual hope is that I'll learn one more tidbit, one more morsel, about the making of this film, the one that indelibly changed who I was forever.

Time Magazine's 'Super Shark' issue from 1975 provided some of the first glimpses behind the curtain of this masterpiece and highlighted the artists and technicians who contributed to this timeless adventure. Now, I'm very proud to say that one of the men responsible for the creation of JAWS is opening his archives to us WITH UNPRECEDENTED ACCESS. That man is named Joe Alves. It turns out that I knew who Joe Alves was when I was growing up without ever having seen a photo of him nor having read an interview with him. He was the production designer on JAWS… and on Close Encounters of the Third Kind, and on John Carpenter's Escape from New York.

A production designer's responsibility, first and foremost, is to visualize what's on the script page. Out of the gate, they are tasked with determining the how, what, and why of the look of the film and subsequently how the production is laid out… finding real locations to match the story, determining what sets need to be built and, in this case, helping a studio figure out how to create a twenty-five-foot man-eating shark.

Today, there would be no hesitation: "Let's do it digitally," would be the response, this to the glee of physical production folks and to the groans of technicians whose imaginations and creative drive would feel stifled. But in 1974 there were no other avenues to pursue and, thanks to the film's maverick director, in order for it to feel real… it had to BE REAL. That meant shooting on the ocean, NOT in a studio tank, and coordinating dozens of effects technicians in an endeavor that had never been attempted before. This task fell on Joe Alves.

Thankfully, those herculean efforts, as tortuous as they may have been, resulted in a piece of film that inspired countless thousands of moviegoers, me being one of them. It was my admiration for Joe and his army of dedicated sculptors, mold-makers, and technicians that ultimately directed me into the field that I love and have been honored to be a part of for the last thirty-four years (and counting). I am proud to call Joe my very good friend and I still sit in awe of his massive artistic talent and ingenuity every time I see him.

RIGHT / Greg Nicotero (far right) with Joe Alves (center) and JAWS special effects technician, Roy Arbogast (far left), flanking Nicotero's faithful recreation of "Bruce," the great white shark.

PREFACE
BY DENNIS L. PRINCE

JAWS WAS THE MOVIE I WAS TOO AFRAID TO SEE.

In early July of 1975, at the age of twelve, I went to see William Castle's *BUG* with a friend. After the show, I feigned at how frightening it was (it really wasn't). My friend, Kevin, remarked, "If you thought that was scary, you should see *JAWS*."

I knew all too well about *JAWS* – the one that may be 'too intense for younger children.' Over the previous four years, I struggled to overcome my fear of monsters, becoming the 'monster kid' of my fifth- and sixth-grade classrooms. "Dennis is so into monsters. He's probably seen all the scary movies out there." So they thought. Mine wasn't a passion so much as a self-prescribed therapy. I mustn't be afraid!

Of course, R-rated fright films were off limits to me (*whew!*), but *JAWS* was offered at an accessible PG rating. So what was I waiting for?

I was scared. I heard it was terrifying. Even the advertisements said so.

I had read the novel; who hadn't by then? I had collected a number of magazines and leaped at an issue of *Reader's Digest* that dared to reveal the truth behind the shriek-inducing shark. Within weeks of the film's June 20, 1975 release, I knew more about *JAWS* than any of my classmates... and yet I still hadn't seen it.

But Kevin's challenge remained. *Why* hadn't I seen the movie? Was I chicken?

Ultimately, I braved a Saturday matinee showing at the Century 24 dome theater on Winchester Boulevard in San Jose, California. Another pal, Danny, was with me; he had already seen it and was there for emotional support (unbeknownst to him). When the house lights went down and the first strains of John Williams' foreboding *da-dummm* seeped through the darkness, I knew I was trapped. There was no escape. Like boarding the ominous Giant Dipper at the Santa Cruz Beach-Boardwalk, once your car left the platform, there was no turning back.

I was scared – you bet – but I was mesmerized, too. When the house lights came up again, I realized I had survived and, in so doing, had discovered the antidote to my fears. Seeing *JAWS* proved to be a transformative experience for me.

My love for film has never waned. When asked, "Dennis, so what's your favorite movie?" without hesitation I answer, "*JAWS*." Now, imagine my

reaction when I found myself sharing a three-hour plane ride seated next to *JAWS* production designer, Joe Alves.

No way! My twelve-year-old mind could never imagine such a possibility. How could a kid like me, who spent hours upon hours reading about *JAWS*, playing the soundtrack album again and again, drawing pictures of the shark, years later be chatting with the man who actually designed the shark I had come to love?

Joe Alves is an amazing person; that's a writer's assessment, not a fan-boy's adoration. His career in film is an elbow-rubbing adventure that rivals the likes of the fictitious Forrest Gump and bears out lineages that outdo Six Degrees of Kevin Bacon. Joe, I soon learned, had been there, done that, and not only 'wore that shirt' but designed it, too! In his forty-some-odd-year career, he had done so much more than I could have ever imagined and he had worked with some of the greats in the industry, on the big and small screens. To my mind, he was practically ubiquitous or omnipresent (Settle down, fan-boy).

I have since become Joe's biographer of record, capturing the span of his amazing work and accompanying him at events and guest appearances where he greets fans and followers just as enthusiastic as I. Regarding *JAWS* specifically, I learned from Joe all that went into designing my favorite film, providing me (and you) another view into the making of the movie. While he can't believe "they're still talking about this movie all these years later," I can believe it because I've come to discover momentous events such as this have a wide spectrum of stories, all dependent upon the point-of-view of those telling them. Director Steven Spielberg has a view that's compelling. Carl Gottlieb (actor and famed writer of *The JAWS Log*) has a slightly different view that is as captivating. The actors all have views that have enthralled us. Now, Joe Alves' own view sheds even more light on this production that people simply can't stop talking about and, without doubt, can't get enough of.

So here it is, Joe Alves' own tales of *Designing JAWS*, revealed through his own art, actions, and anecdotes. And here I am, the lucky kid who gets to share all that I've learned through my remarkable good fortune to have become a collaborator with and friend to the man.

And, in case you're wondering – yes, I'm listening to the *JAWS* soundtrack as I write this.

BELOW / In 1975, a 12-year-old boy courageously embarks upon a transformative movie-going experience.

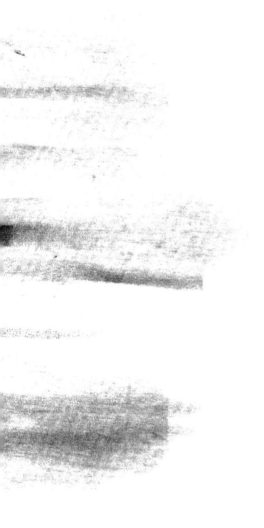

INTRODUCTION

IN THE SUMMER OF 1973, if someone yelled "shark," the response would likely be "What? Where? What does it look like?" Ironically, just as 1973 would see the signing of the Endangered Species Act, few Americans had considered what might happen if a certain species – specifically, sharks – would indiscriminately endanger *us*.

And, in 1973, the word 'jaws' hadn't any real meaning beyond our own hinged mandible. It was a harmless word; it didn't mean much of anything to anyone... except, perhaps, to a first-time novelist, his literary agent, and a publisher... oh, and an erudite magazine-editor-turned-movie-producer with a sharp eye for juicy material.

The novelist, Peter Benchley, wondered what might happen if a large predator – *a great white shark* – were to station itself off the coast of a sleepy little island in the Atlantic Ocean, staking claim to it as its private feeding ground, well stocked with unaware bathers – fleshy, soft, delicious. Would a 'dumb fish' do such a thing? A premise like this hadn't been suggested to the masses in any sort of widespread, none-of-us-is-safe alarm. But through this exploit, Benchley offered each of us something more disturbing to consider: while happily paddling through the water, do we know what might be silently following along beneath?

As for the novel's simple four-letter title, that was bred through happenstance by Benchley's recounting of an exasperated exchange with his agent as the two argued over a suitable title; they argued over naming it jaws-of-this or jaws-of-that, but never finding agreement.

"We cannot agree on a single word that we like let alone a title that we like. In fact, the only word that even means anything, that even says anything, is 'jaws.' Call the book 'JAWS.'"

And with that, a new four-letter word would be unleashed within our popular culture. It meant nothing yet but soon it would become synonymous with horror and helplessness, striking terror in hearts and minds of anyone who dared to venture into untamed waters. Ultimately, *JAWS* would do for the oceans what Alfred Hitchcock's *Psycho* did for the shower. Are you safe?

So, today, when we think of sharks, we now instinctively think of *JAWS*. When we hear the word "jaws," we naturally think of sharks. Peter Benchley's novel became the cultural phenomenon of the bookshelf. Upon its release in February 1974, it was evident that *JAWS* had teeth. It claimed a territory atop the *New York Times* bestseller list and would remain there for a full forty-four weeks. Early reaction indicated that *JAWS* could strike a primal chord with readers everywhere. Publisher Doubleday Press, having wisely anticipated the book's commercial potential, proactively staged pre-publication campaigns with book clubs, critics, and relevant periodicals of the day. That's when *Cosmopolitan* editor-in-chief Helen Gurley Brown passed along the early galley sheets to husband and movie producer David Brown, with a note attached:

Might make a good movie...

Brown knew movie material. Hired in 1951 by legendary producer Darryl F. Zanuck to head the story department at 20th Century Fox, Brown rose to become the executive vice-president of creative operations at the studio. After two decades at Fox, Brown and newfound business partner, Richard D. Zanuck (son of Darryl) left Fox to establish themselves as motion picture producers. Their first co-produced picture, a tepid horror-of-nature thriller called *Sssssss*, was released in July of 1973, just as final preparations were being made for the release of their next film, *The Sting*, before year's end. Simultaneous to that, shooting of their third feature, *The Sugarland Express*, had just completed and was in the hands of film editors Ed Abroms and Verna Fields, who were accompanied by the film's energetic young director, Steven Spielberg.

When Brown received the pre-publication galley sheets for Benchley's *JAWS* during the summer of 1973, the wily producer acted quickly. He rang up Universal Studios to connect with Joe Alves, the studio art director who had just completed work with Spielberg and production manager Bill Gilmore on

The Sugarland Express. Brown said he'd send along the galley sheets of Benchley's manuscript, asking Alves to illustrate the key action sequences for use as a pitch for a film adaptation. If pitched properly, Brown figured Universal's head of production, Marshall Green, would surely bite.

And so it began. There wouldn't be much expectation for this *JAWS* project, outside of it being just a "quick summer popcorn movie" (as the film's co-screenwriter and actor Carl Gottlieb recounts). Since the novel hadn't yet been published, it was a gamble. Benchley was an unknown. His novel was an unknown. Sharks were... well... not unknown but nobody was talking much about them in those days.

A what? Where? What does it look like?

As a modest endeavor, *JAWS* would likely be categorized as just a 'monster movie,' one in competition with heady science-fiction extravaganzas like *2001: A Space Odyssey*, *Silent Running*, and *Soylent Green*. Beyond those, the wildly popular 'disaster pictures' were top draw at the box office – *The Poseidon Adventure*, *The Towering Inferno*, and Universal's own catastrophe contender, *Earthquake*.

Amid this competition, *JAWS* would need to be different, both on the screen and within the public consciousness, if it would stand any chance to draw in moviegoers. It would have to resonate with audiences with an unsettling delivery that could effectively drop them into the unimaginable predicament of being afloat in the water with an insatiable 'eating machine' circling below.

So could this be more than just a summertime monster movie? If the book succeeded, could it draw in avid readers (and those not inclined to read) to see Benchley's terrors unfold before their eyes? And, if done properly, could it deliver the same sort of unnerving realism that had moviegoers lining up along city blocks as seen with wildly successful novel adaptations like *The Godfather* and *The Exorcist*? *JAWS* – a 'blockbuster'? Could be...

PREVIOUS SPREAD / Joe Alves' early charcoal sketch of the unstoppable great white predator.

RIGHT / Joe Alves' charcoal sketch unleashes *JAWS* upon the world.

JOE ALVES
PRODUCTION DESIGNER

A PRODUCTION DESIGNER'S WORK is a mystery to many people. Its value and impact to a motion picture is often misunderstood and frequently overlooked. While so many of us love 'the movies,' not all are enlightened regarding to the actual 'art' of filmmaking and the indispensible contributions of these specialized artists in particular, the production designers.

The long-used notion of 'movie magic' implies that, over the course of a film, we will see sights that lead us through visual narratives that cause us to suspend disbelief, accepting what we're seeing and, when the design is executed properly, becoming fully immersed in the world that is revealed to us on the movie screen. And so just as a stage magician is tasked to make us believe in the incredible tricks and illusions he performs, all the while careful to never reveal the technical methods he employs to achieve his trickery, the same goes for production designers; they present places, settings, and situations we assume were simply 'found' (lucky that) but, in truth, were carefully constructed to make us believe they are real. That's the trick – the technical illusion – that the production designer performs.

But the production designer's work isn't staged trickery – it's art. Production design requires a unique ability to see what isn't there (consider the painter's blank canvas) and then visualize how to render something for the camera to capture. It requires insightful interpretation, painstaking planning, and skillful execution. When done right, it convinces audiences that what they're seeing is real. It's the art of the illusion. It's movie magic. It's the craft of the production designer.

The production designer's first duty is to present artistic expressions that convey a look, a mood, a tone, and a visual voice for a production, all that can be executed in a believable way within the context and structure of a film. But before setting about to

convince an audience, the production designer must first convince those with whom he or she will work: that is, the team of filmmakers who'll collaborate to conceive, construct, and deliver a film that will engage, entrance, and even inspire those who see the finished product. The production designer uses illustrations, models, and various other mock-ups to establish a harmonious collaboration among the film's director, its scriptwriter, its photographer, and the complement of other crew members – and don't forget the actors themselves – in a way that all who are involved will develop a shared vision of what the film can be, what it wants to be, and what it needs to be (that's usually driven by studio executives or other anxious stakeholders).

BELOW / Joe Alves' charcoal drawing that ultimately resulted in an actor's most celebrated ad-libbed line, "You're gonna need a bigger boat..."

ABOVE / Joe Alves inspects the skeletal foundation of the great white shark. Note the full-scale drawing on the back wall.

At the outset, the production design conveys what the writer had imagined; it enables the director to tell the film story as he or she sees fit; it presents the settings that the photographer can effectively capture on film; it gives the actors the environments they need to perform within. It's all achieved by the experienced production designer through his presentation of the creative elements that explain how the production will look and, in so doing, will inspire all involved to make the production a worthwhile and believable endeavor, technically as well as artistically.

So when Joe Alves stepped into the role of production designer for a film named *JAWS*, he was bringing his twenty years of experience to the job. *JAWS* would be his newest canvas upon which he would again practice and further refine his movie-magic artistry.

Joe Alves began working in the film and television industry from an early age. He started as an 'In-Betweener' animator at Walt Disney Studios at age nineteen, securing that job almost accidentally (he hoped he could maybe land a summer appointment sweeping up around the place) thanks to a solid portfolio of his high school art and design work. He quickly moved up to a position of assistant animator, working with effects pioneer Joshua Meador in animating the unique 'Id' encounter in MGM's *Forbidden Planet* of 1956. He would next work on several sequences for Disney's 1957 animated feature, *Sleeping Beauty*. But, as much as he liked animation, he developed a desire to work in live action.

Alves left Disney, electing to work on stage productions at the modest Hollywood Playhouse, a small venue where he could manage set design and stage dressing. Satisfied with his work yet always looking for his next upward opportunity, he turned to Hollywood's studio circuit with aspirations of becoming an art director for feature films. That journey began with a position as a junior set designer for ZIV Television Productions, giving him need and reason to hone his technical drafting skills. That job would gain him a host of assignments in the drafting room where he worked on design specifications for TV and movie productions from 20th Century Fox (*From the Terrace*) and MGM (*How the West Was Won*, *My Fair Lady*).

Next, Alves moved on to Universal Studios where, as senior set designer, he worked on Stanley Kramer's *It's a Mad, Mad, Mad, Mad World*. Advancing to assistant art director, he worked on Alfred Hitchcock's *Torn Curtain* (yes, he discussed details of set design with the legendary director).

At Universal, Alves excelled under the tutelage of accomplished art director, Frank Arrigo, who admired young Alves' work ethic, willingness to learn, and ability to adapt to compressed shooting schedules while delivering creative designs. Next, Alves accepted assignments on Universal's many television series and made-for-TV movies (the sort at which most of the long-time designers would turn up their prideful noses). For Alves, the shift in direction paid off handsomely: he gained the desired position of art director for *Rod Serling's Night Gallery* series. Ultimately, that three-season duty led him back to feature films where he was assigned as art director for *The Sugarland Express*, which brought the feature-film debut of budding young director Steven Spielberg and was backed by emerging powerhouse producers, Richard D. Zanuck and David Brown.

Production manager Bill Gilmore, heading up the *Sugarland* project, paid a visit to the studio's acting head of art in charge of television productions, Bill DeCinces. "I need an art director for a new picture," Gilmore said, "one we'll be shooting on location with a young director, Steven Spielberg. What we really need is a young Frank Arrigo."

DeCinces smiled.

"You want Joe Alves," DeCinces offered, recalling commendations from Arrigo himself. "I think he's exactly what you're looking for – and he's worked with Spielberg before."

Indeed, Alves and Spielberg had a brief collaboration on a short-lived television series, *The Psychiatrist*, Alves as art director and Spielberg as director. It made sense the two would again collaborate on the *Sugarland* picture. And after *Sugarland*, of course, would come *JAWS*.

So with two decades of design experience to his credit, Alves had earned what he needed most for this next assignment: collaborative credentials and creative confidence. He was solid in his artistic ability, well practiced in navigating the production process,

UNIVERSAL CITY STUDIOS, INC.

AN MCA INC. COMPANY

JOSEPH ALVES
ART DIRECTOR

100 UNIVERSAL CITY PLAZA
UNIVERSAL CITY, CALIF. 91608
(213) 985-4321

and cleverly creative in maximizing the value of his output under the constraints of a budget (in both time and money). And, although he had achieved recognition as an art director, he was eager to move up to the next rung in film design: production designer.

What's the distinction between art director and production designer? That came with 1939's *Gone with the Wind* when producer David O. Selznick bestowed the title of 'production designer' upon William Cameron Menzies, largely out of sheer gratitude for Menzies' saving of the epic production whose look and style had previously become an unmanageable nightmare. Menzies, with his experience in both design and direction, established a compelling look, tone, and feel for Selznick's mismanaged production, ultimately making it a cinematic masterpiece of design. As such, Selznick offered this special credit to Menzies:

This Production Designed by William Cameron Menzies

Although Alves wasn't imagining *Gone with the Wind* accolades, he was nonetheless committed to bringing his best effort to every production. "We never slacked on our approach," he assured. "Even though no one had yet heard of *JAWS* – the book still hadn't been published when I started work on it – it was a challenge and an opportunity, just like every production would be."

Joe Alves would put the 'first boots on the ground' in the making of *JAWS*. As the art director (soon-to-be-named production designer), he would begin visualizing Benchley's terrors. He'd tour coastlines in search of the unsuspecting Amity Island. He'd find colors, feel textures, and pinpoint settings that could lull audiences into a short-lived sense of serenity, only to plunge them into a nightmare world where a voracious monster glides silently below the waterline.

In his first days on the *JAWS* assignment, there was no anticipation for this adventure; there was no widespread worry nor wonder about great white sharks; and there was no recognition of a da-dum, da-dum musical cue that signaled imminent danger.

At the very beginning, there was only an unpublished novel called *JAWS* and an art director named Joe Alves.

RIGHT / Joe Alves on location overseeing the execution of his designs for *JAWS*.

CONCEIVING THE CARNAGE

THE PRODUCTION DESIGNER'S JOB is to visualize the contents, concepts, and context of a narrative for translation into a work of film. No matter if the work is to be historically accurate or fantastically fictitious, the work must embody the essence and impact that a screenwriter, a director, a producer, or whoever else is financing the project expects to see. This is a sort of 'proof-of-concept' phase to determine if the project really has legs (or fins).

So when David Brown's curiosity was piqued by Peter Benchley's manuscript, he immediately wanted two things: 1) a visualization of how the novel's events could be depicted on film and, 2) an engaging presentation that would compel a movie studio to buy it. It was at that time that he made a phone call to Joe Alves.

"He said he was sending over galley sheets for a new book," Alves recalls, "and asked if I would make some illustrations of the 'action sequences'; he said I'd know them when I read them. As it wasn't an official studio project yet, I didn't have the usual charge number to bill my time to. That's when Brown asked that I 'just squeeze it in, please.' David Brown wasn't the sort of producer you turn down, so I did it."

THIS SPREAD / Joe Alves begins his design conceptualization by illustrating (and thereby understanding) the taxonomy and temperament of the great white shark.

Alves knew nothing of sharks, but was captivated by the premise that Benchley presented. Immediately, he began researching sharks, how they look, how they move, and then he began drawing them based on the photos he was seeing. He acquainted himself with their shape, their curves, and then extrapolated that into more threatening renderings.

After reading the novel's galley sheets, Alves easily found the key sequences that David Brown had alluded to during their phone conversation: the various shark attacks and the confrontations between the three main characters and the monstrous beast. Benchley provided ample detail of the gruesome assaults bracketed by taut suspense that kept the narrative engaging and irresistible.

With just pencil and paper, Alves made preliminary sketches of some of the sequences, again to ensure he was confident in how to illustrate the shark, how to properly represent the size of the fish in relation to the humans (it would be as big as Benchley asserted), and, most important, how to establish the drama, suspense, and terror that would need to be captured on film. This was to be a pitch so it had to convince Brown as well as the studio people that *JAWS* had potential. Alves was baiting the hook; Brown would cast the line; both would hope the studio people would bite.

Alves will be quick to say that he's not of the same artistic caliber as those designers and illustrators whom he has admired over the years: Dale Hennesey, John DeCuir, and Ken Adam. Nevertheless, he's confident in his own work as well as his ability to capture not only what will fit within the film frame but also how to present it from a point of view that provides dramatic impact.

"As I was progressing along in my design career, my mentor, Frank Arrigo, gave to me a key piece of advice. 'Joe,' he said, 'when you design, don't think like a designer; think like a director.' In that, he was explaining that a good designer approaches his work with a director's eye, helping to solve some of the challenges of filming a sequence by applying design principles to get the most effective shots. I applied that approach to my television work and now I was applying it to the film work."

Alves heeded Arrigo's advice when illustrating Benchley's action, especially given that, at that time, there was no director assigned to the project – because it wasn't yet a 'project.' So with sheets of vellum paper and his artists' charcoals (a preferred medium of his), he began rendering the various sequences, giving life to Benchley's horrors, working quietly in his office at the Universal Studios art department as he envisioned the novel brought to screen.

RIGHT / Joe Alves begins illustrating Peter Benchley's marauding maneater.

JAWS

Peter Benchley

1974

DOUBLEDAY & COMPANY, INC., GARDE?

FIRST WOULD BE THE ATTACK on Chrissie Watkins, who ventures into the nighttime ocean, unaware of what is stalking her from beneath. Benchley used the jarring sequence to quickly capture his readers; Alves would do so, likewise, to entice and hook the Universal team.

Stark and startling, the opening sequence epitomized the terror of the unseen while unflinchingly exploiting the primal fear of a brutal and unexpected assault which culminates in the unimaginable experience of being eaten alive. It effectively sets the tone for the events to come.

Considering the technical side of the opening proposition, Alves' first set of illustrations also demonstrated the need to develop a giant predator effect, one that can be manipulated for the camera (ruling out the initial notion that, perhaps, sharks can be trained to perform like dolphins and killer whales; they can't). But this was only the first attack; the next would be far more unsettling and likely more difficult to execute on film.

THIS PAGE / Chrissie Watkins enjoys a nighttime swim in the ocean, unaware of the terror that is swimming with her.

RIGHT / From Peter Benchley's *JAWS*: "...the fish shook its head from side to side, its serrated triangular teeth sawing through what little sinew still resisted."

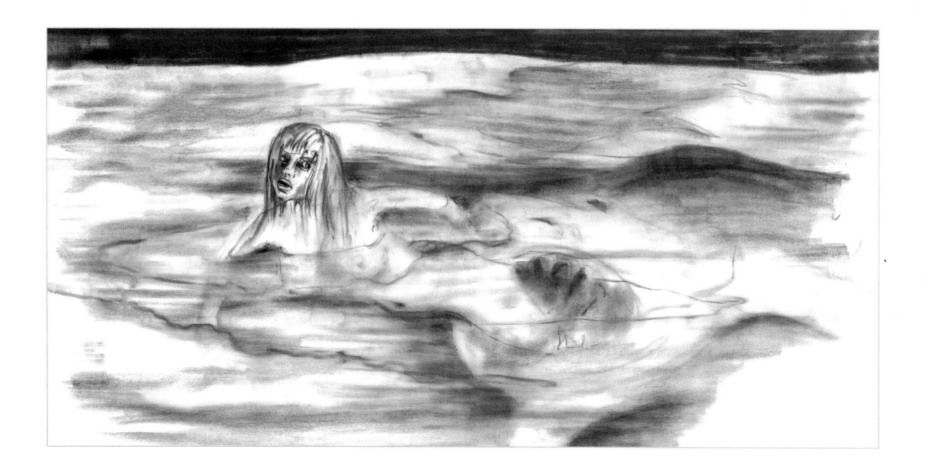

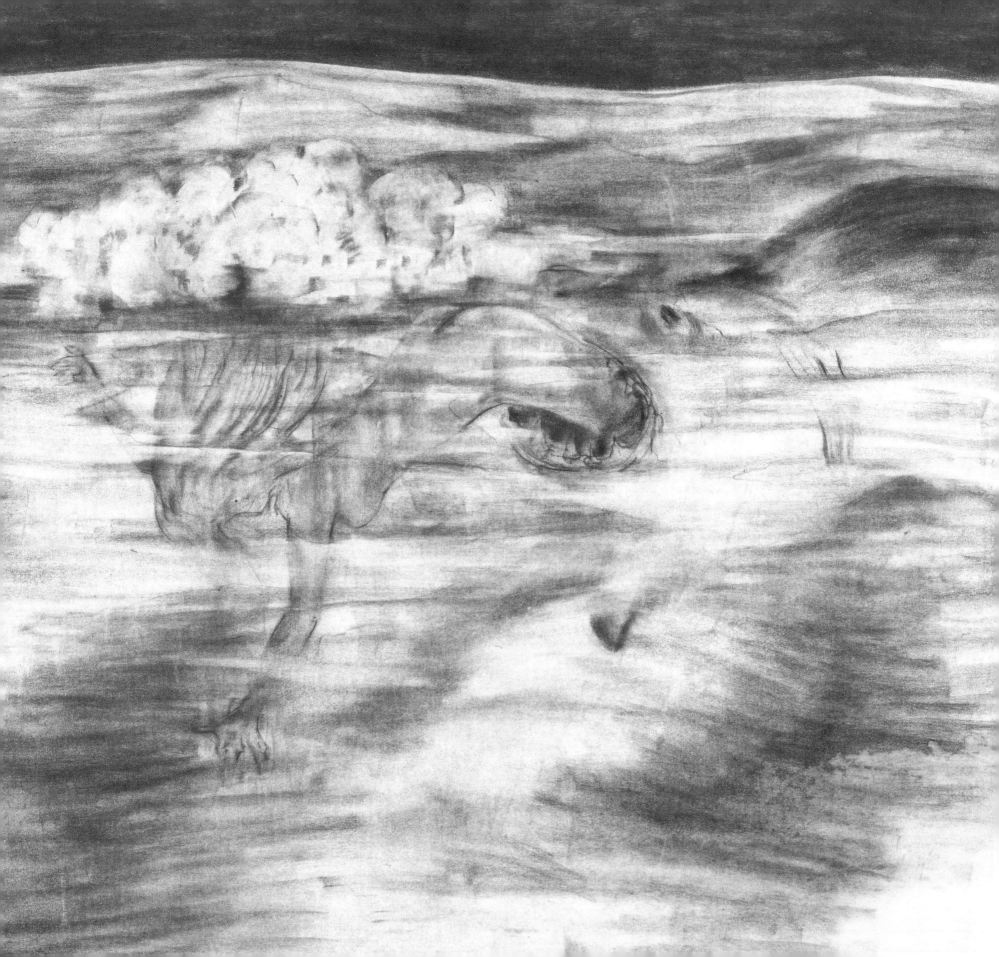

AS IF TO WILLINGLY VEER into the realm of the unspeakable, Benchley next describes an attack on a six-year-old boy, doe-eyed Alex Kintner, who stubbornly nags his mother to let him paddle his inflatable raft out onto the waves; he promises he'll stay within easy sight.

As Benchley writes it, the boy's innocence is matched by a certain cunning when, seeing he's not gaining the permission he desires, he unfairly makes reference to an absent father: "I bet Dad would let me," comes the child's ruthless ploy. Mom relents

and the boy happily paddles away into the surf, both of them unaware of what's lurking offshore.

Mom should have stood firm.

In his illustrating of the Kintner attack, Alves matched Benchley's unblanched aplomb, graphically depicting the behemoth shark stalking an innocent and wholly helpless child from beneath the water's surface; the suspense is palpable. The ultimate attack is stunning, not only in its need for complex execution but also in its complications of good taste and moral rightness.

THIS SPREAD / "Can we really show a kid being eaten on screen?!"

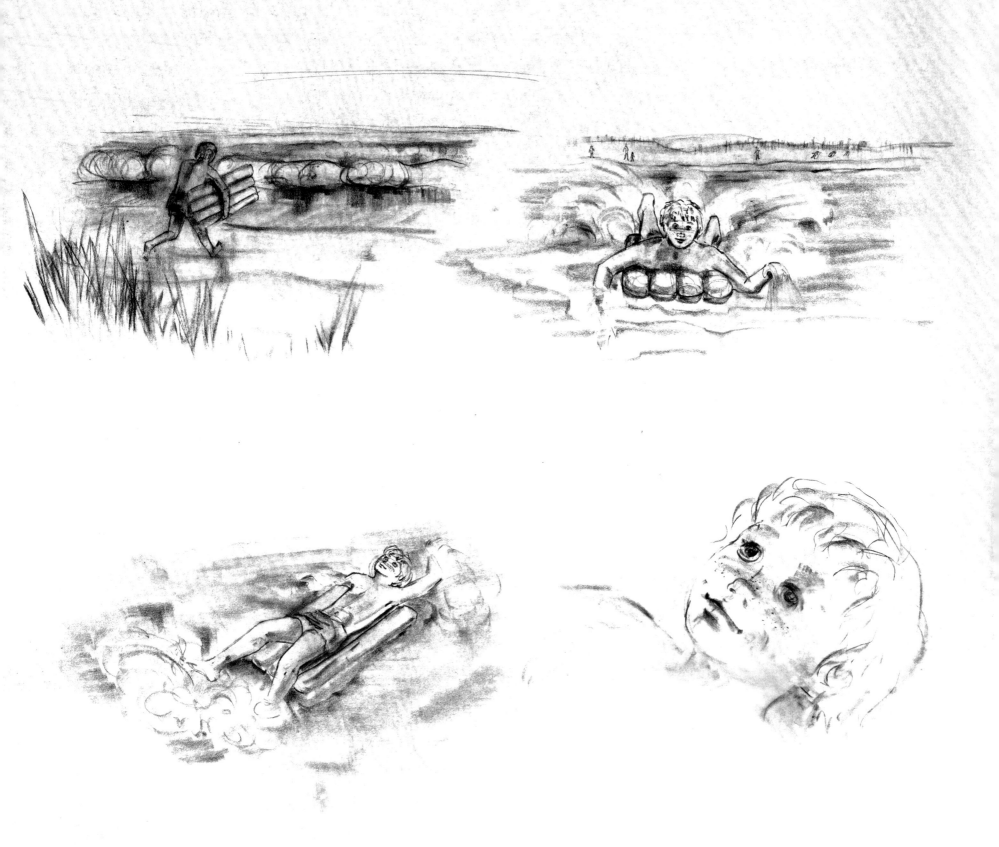

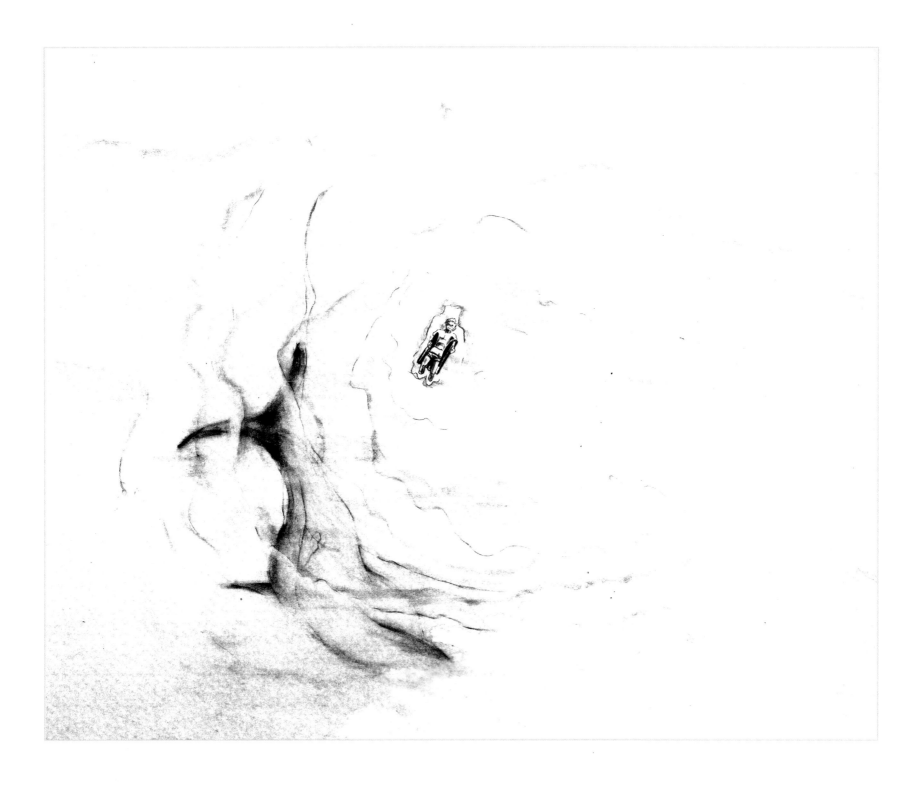

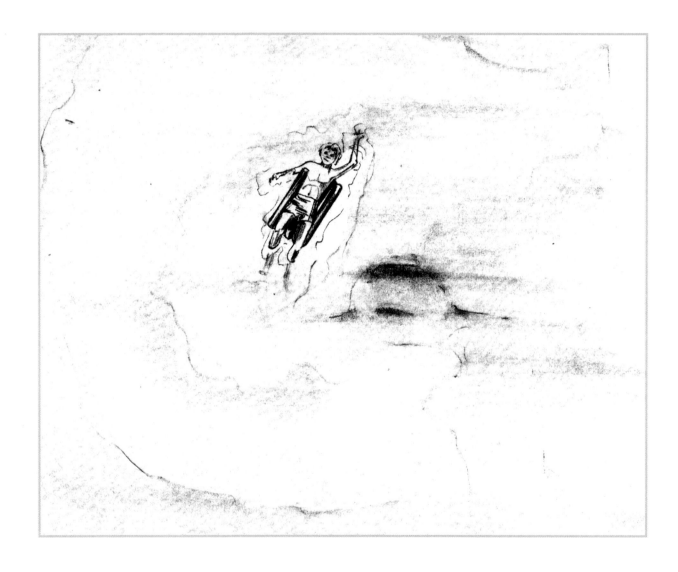

THE ATTACK ON LOCAL FISHERMAN Ben Gardner posed a different sort of challenge to Alves in that Benchley doesn't describe the event anywhere in his prose. Rather, it is an attack that occurs 'off camera.' Chief of Police Martin Brody and the island's mayor, Larry Vaughan, quietly dispatch Gardner to find and kill the shark before the island community learns of the recent deaths. Later, Brody spots Gardner's boat adrift and investigates with his deputy. While they don't find Gardner, they do find evidence that he has likely become yet another victim of the menacing shark. Alves, then, was tasked to imagine and illustrate what might have happened to the missing fisherman.

The technical challenge in executing the Ben Gardner attack would be devising a way to show a full-bodied shark that crests the ocean surface and literally leaps across the bow of the boat, swallowing the hapless fisherman whole.

THIS SPREAD / Joe Alves ambitiously envisions the massive great white shark emerging in full sight to take the doomed fisherman.

MAYOR VAUGHAN NOW AGREES to Chief Brody's appeal to hire the caustic Quint, a professional 'sharker' who barks his assurance that he can find and kill the great white shark. Brody, along with the unflinching yet largely untried oceanographer, Matt Hooper, set out to sea aboard Quint's weathered vessel, the *Orca*.

A first day of slopping ladlefuls of fish blood and entrails (a wretched mix called 'chum') into the ocean is uneventful, save for establishing the three on-board personalities who immediately grate on one another. A second day of chum line finally lures the great white alongside the *Orca*, revealing itself to be a twenty-five-foot monster. The fish, it seems, studies the trio as much as they study it. Brody is fearful. Hooper is fascinated. Quint is simply fixated on completing his business and collecting his bounty. But this shark is smart, deftly removing bait from Quint's hook without a chance for the crusty sharker

to so much as snag it. The trio heads back to dock, somewhat more encouraged than the day before yet still empty-handed.

Before setting off for a third day of the hunt, Hooper arranges for an anti-shark cage to be loaded onto the *Orca*. Quint objects, not so much in concern over the extra weight to his vessel but, rather, to the sheer audacity (or stupidity) of Hooper believing he'd be safe in a veritable wire box dangled in front of the mammoth shark. Hooper persists and the cage is loaded on board. A fresh chum line attracts the shark, but the shark, this time provokes its would-be captors by ramming the boat's keel then quickly retreating (as if baiting the three hunters). In an effort to pique the shark's curiosity, the men lower Hooper's cage into the water. Then, to satisfy his own curiosity, Hooper lowers himself into the cage in hopes of further inspecting and photographing the shark. The great white approaches and unleashes its savage fury.

THIS SPREAD / Alves' sketch illustrates an undeniable helplessness as Hooper will find he is mismatched against the massive shark.

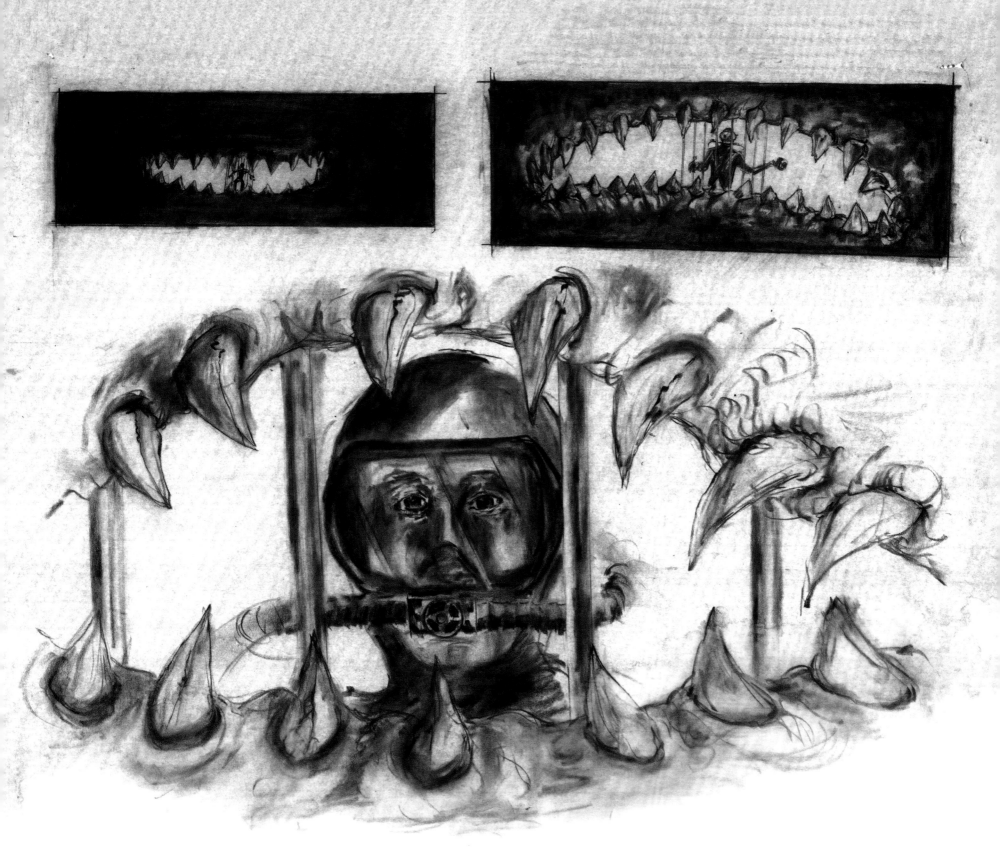

THIS SPREAD / Alves' inventive vision for the shark's approach on Hooper as seen from inside the *JAWS*.

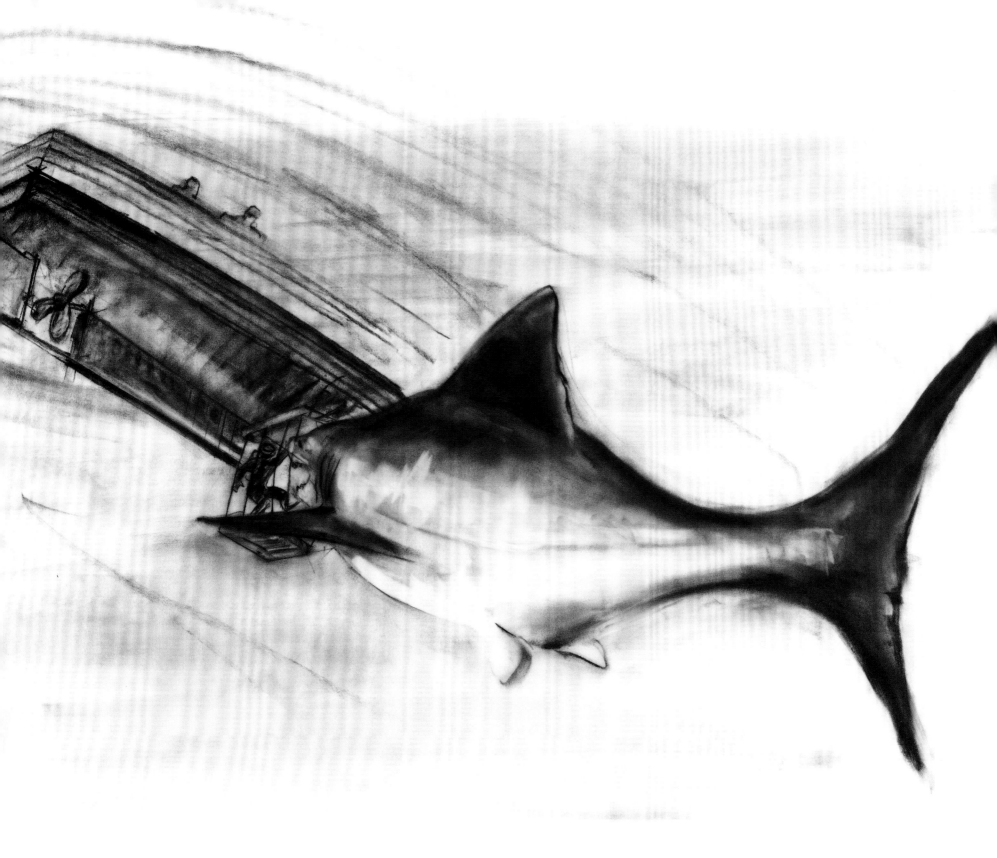

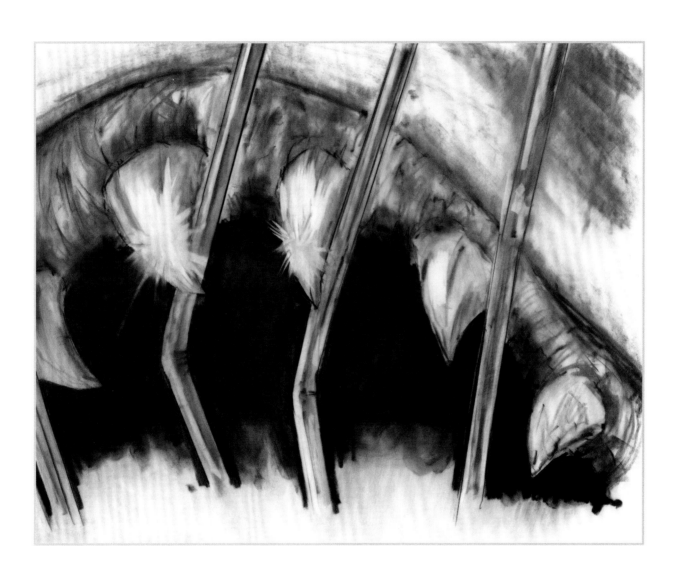

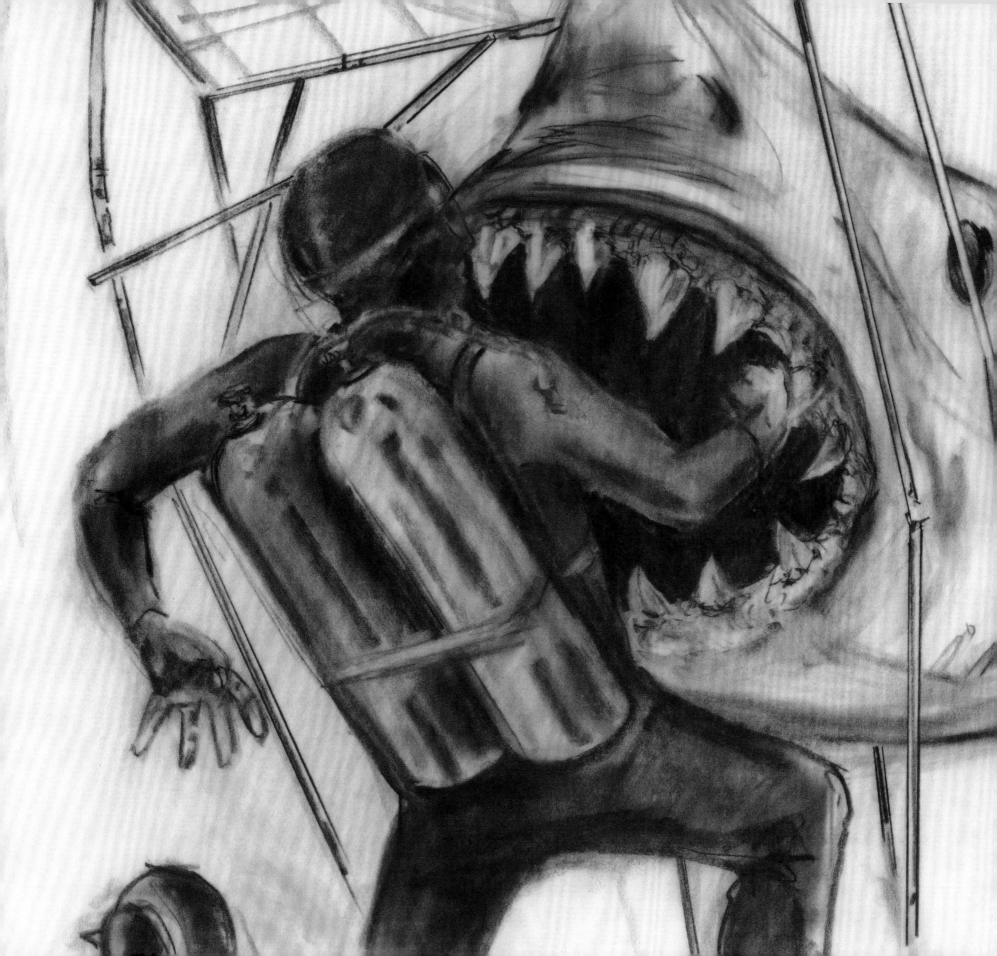

❚❚ The fish thrust again, and Hooper saw with the terror of doom that the mouth was going to reach him." *PETER BENCHLEY'S JAWS*

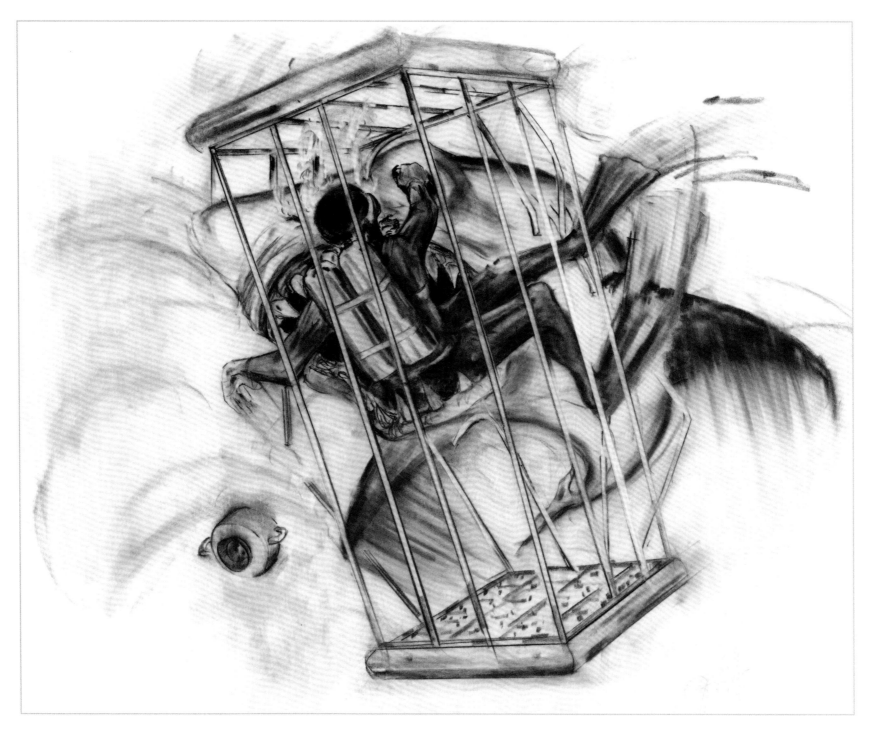

ABOVE / "The jaws closed around his torso. Hooper felt a terrible pressure, as if his guts were being compacted."

ABOVE / "Hooper's body protruded from each side of the mouth, head and arms hanging limply down one side, knees, calves, and feet from the other."

WHILE HOOPER'S DEATH HAS LEFT BRODY DISTRAUGHT, it serves to only harden Quint's resolve to catch and kill this unnatural foe. Using harpoons and barrels, Quint aims to weaken the shark, then he'll angle for the killing shot. The next day on the ocean would prove to be one of final confrontation for all – the unsteady police chief, the enraged sharker, and the seemingly unstoppable great white terror.

The battle between man and fish pushes all to their limits. Every ounce of Quint's skill and cunning seems to fall short of being able to subdue the sea beast. The shark itself, likely sensing it has met its match, throws itself onto the deck of the *Orca* in a desperate attempt to survive the onslaught of the harpoons and barrels. In the melee, Quint is tangled in the ropes from his harpoons and dragged below the water's surface by the severely weakened yet still-advancing great white.

After the shark takes Quint below the water's surface to his doom, Brody prepares for his own death at the jaws of the oncoming killer… and then the shark stops, rolls to one side, and sinks into the depths. The toll of Quint's harpoons and barrels has finally defeated it.

So, with more than forty charcoal illustrations completed, Joe Alves was prepared to meet with the Universal executives and special effects team to tell Benchley's tale and, more importantly, to begin determining how they'd go about putting it to film.

THIS SPREAD / The final confrontation will be a thrilling battle between man and monster. If executed correctly, it could be a triumph in filmmaking.

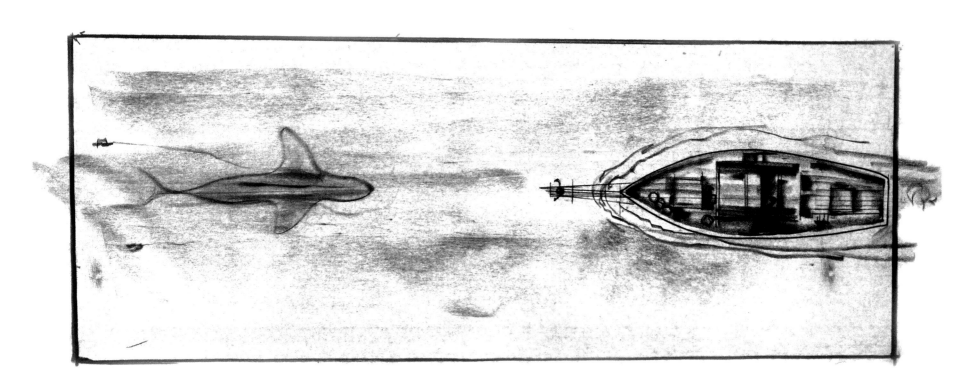

ABOVE / As unrelenting as the shark, Quint assails the beast with harpoons and barrels to exhaust and overcome his adversary.

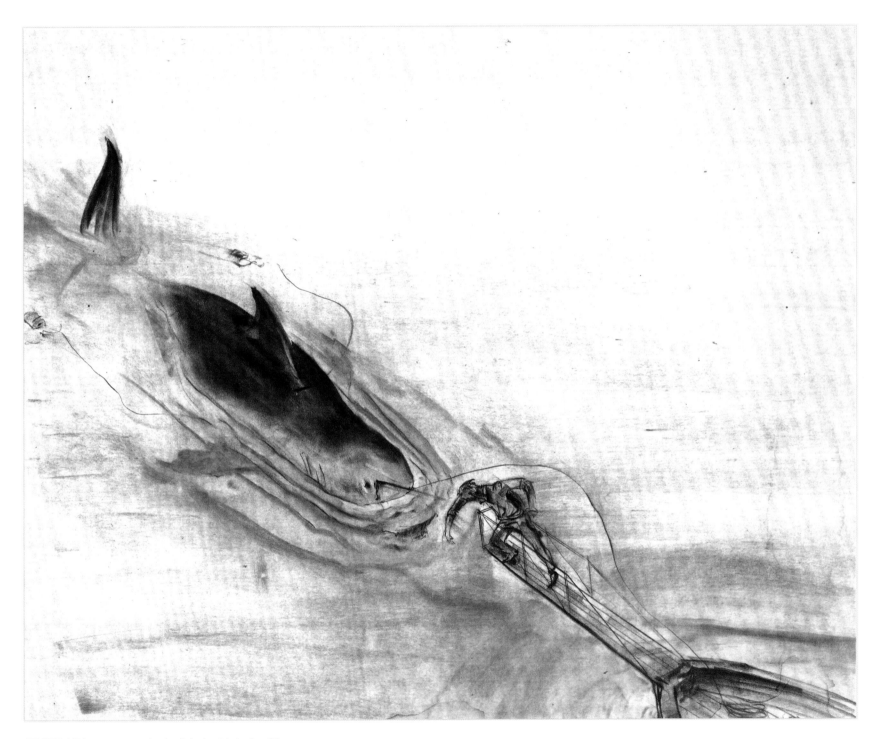

ABOVE / "Have you ever had a fish do this before?"

ABOVE / "The sonofabitch is coming up!"

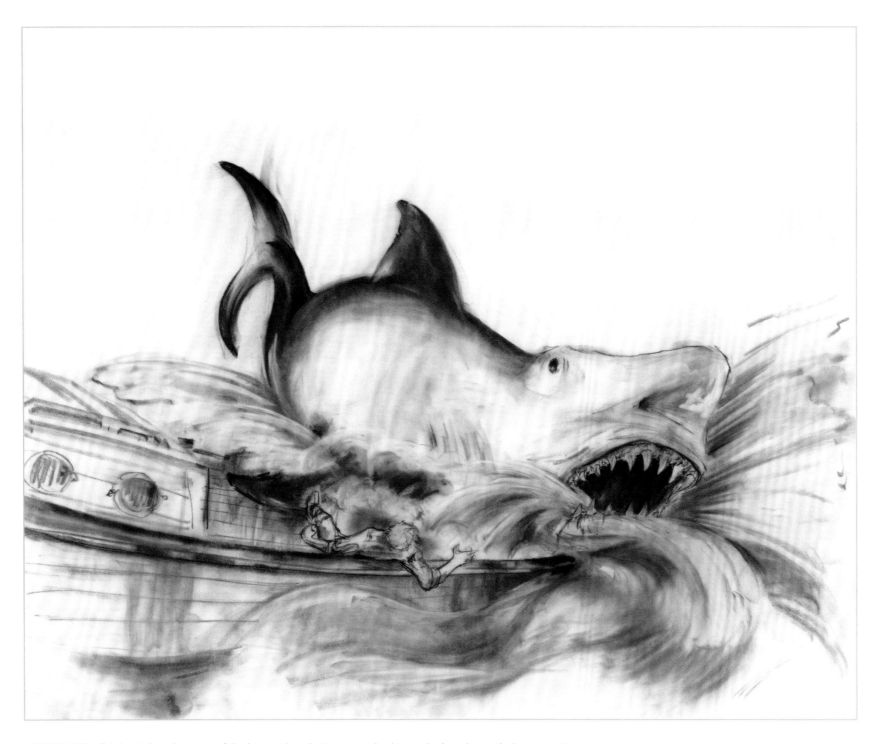

ABOVE / "The fish landed on the stern of the boat with a shattering crash, driving the boat beneath the waves."

ABOVE / "The fish lay there, its jaw not three feet from Brody's chest."

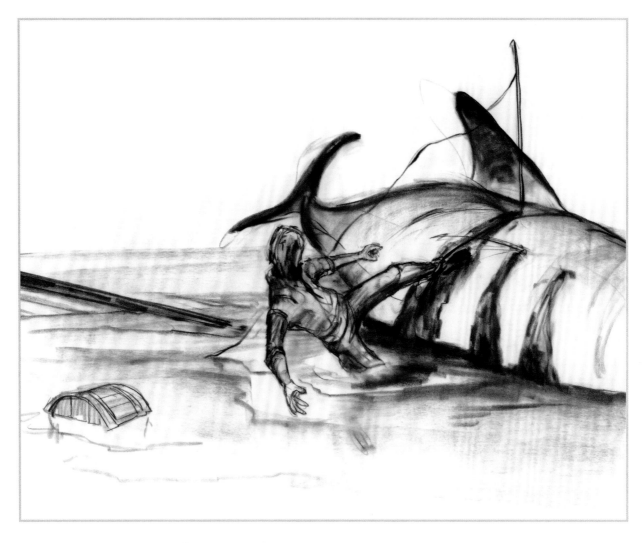

THIS SPREAD / "The fish rolled off the stern and slid beneath the waves. Brody saw the rope coiled around Quint's foot."

FAR LEFT / "[Brody] closed his eyes, waiting for an agony he could not imagine."

LEFT / "...as Brody watched, the steel-gray body began to recede downward into the gloom."

HOW TO MAKE A MANEATER

"BUT THAT'S NEVER BEEN DONE!"

The reaction from Universal's head of special effects, 'Punky' Chinque, was as vehement as it was dismissive.

Joe Alves had just finished presenting his concept drawings, explaining the actions required of the shark effect. What he had just described, by Chinque's estimation, and agreed to by Orien Ernest, also representing the special effects department, was beyond complex. It had never been done before and would surely take years to develop.

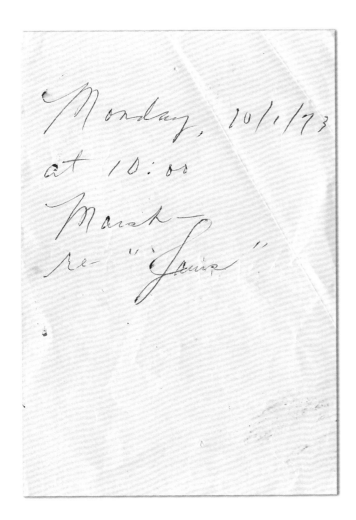

ABOVE / A meeting in Marshall Green's office to discuss a new film project.

ABOVE / The Black Tower.

"We don't have years," Marshall Green countered to Chinque's stalling. "This could be really big for us – *all of us* – and for the studio!"

All in attendance shifted a bit nervously in their chairs. As elegant as was Green's well-appointed meeting room positioned high within Universal's glistening and imposing Black Tower, it was nonetheless his turf – he earned it and you damned well better respect it.

"Well, right now we can't get to it any sooner," Chinque continued, cautiously. "You know we're already wrapped up on *The Hindenburg* and *Earthquake*–"

"*JAWS* could be a bigger movie than *Earthquake* or *The Hindenburg*," Green interjected, slamming his hand on the table. Chinque wisely stifled a snicker at Green's assertion.

Alves quietly rolled his collection of drawings.

Steven Spielberg sat quietly, pondering Green's assertion that *JAWS* could be bigger than *The Hindenburg*. He and Alves had already been schooled over the fact that real sharks can't be trained to perform, not like dolphins or killer whales. They agreed they needed some sort of animatronic shark to stage the action, only now it seemed the effects team couldn't – or wouldn't – be of any help.

Bill DeCinces sat comfortably, satisfied with Alves' presentation while, admittedly, also unsure of how such on-screen effects could be achieved. Resorting to miniatures or optical trickery might not be good enough, not for today's increasingly sophisticated and even jaded audiences.

Bill Gilmore, assigned as production executive, also sat quietly but was in no way deterred by Chinque's doubts. Like Green, Gilmore fully believed that this could be a really big picture. He was especially confident in the abilities of Alves and Spielberg, having seen how well they worked on *The Sugarland Express*. He had no doubt that these guys had the proper mix of energy and ambition to make the project work; they just needed the effects department in their corner.

RIGHT / Joe Alves' earliest rough concept sketches.

David Brown sat to the right of Green, his gaze gentle yet thoughtful, as always. Both he and his partner, Richard Zanuck, believed this could be a soundly profitable venture, maybe not of *Hindenburg* or *Earthquake* stature, but with potential nonetheless. And, since the producers were under contract to deliver another picture to Universal, he wasn't inclined to let this one get away.

The silence continued, no one in the room willing to compromise on their current convictions.

"You know," Chinque ventured, "it would be a lot easier if you shoot this in a tank or in the lagoon here on the lot."

"No – no way," Spielberg retorted.

Both he and Alves had already discussed this option, having quickly ruled it out upon screening *The Old Man and the Sea*. It was painful to watch the legendary Spencer Tracy trapped in a studio tank with a phony background and a prop marlin bobbing alongside a little rowboat.

"People will laugh if we try it that way."

"Yeah, we know it won't be easy to do it on the ocean," Alves added, "but if you read the galleys, you'll understand why we need to shoot it on location."

"Well, maybe..." Chinque mused, "but not this year."

The meeting ended.

All rose and exchanged polite smiles, making their way out of the room. Spielberg, Brown, and Zanuck paused momentarily at the doorway, as if tempted to continue a sidebar conversation, then elected not to. They walked out. Now, only Alves and Green remained.

"Joe," Green said, "do you really think this can be done?"

"I do. I don't exactly know how, but I think we can make it happen."

"Take it off the lot, then. See if you can find someone at one of the other studios, someone else who might be able to do it."

Alves' eyes widened. "Oh – OK, I'll do that." It was practically unheard of to be given executive permission to work outside the studio lines, to sidestep the protocol and politics to pursue an external solution, wherever it might exist. "Thanks, Marshall. I'll figure it out."

"Just keep it sort of mum, will you? No need to advertise this, OK?"

"Sure thing." Alves smiled, hiked up his drawings under his arm, and walked out of Green's office.

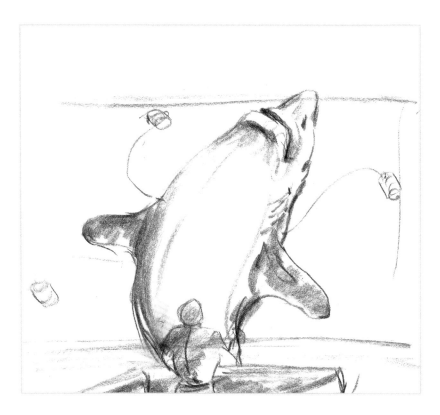

LEFT / An early rough sketch indicates filming should take place in the open ocean.

RIGHT / More early concept sketches.

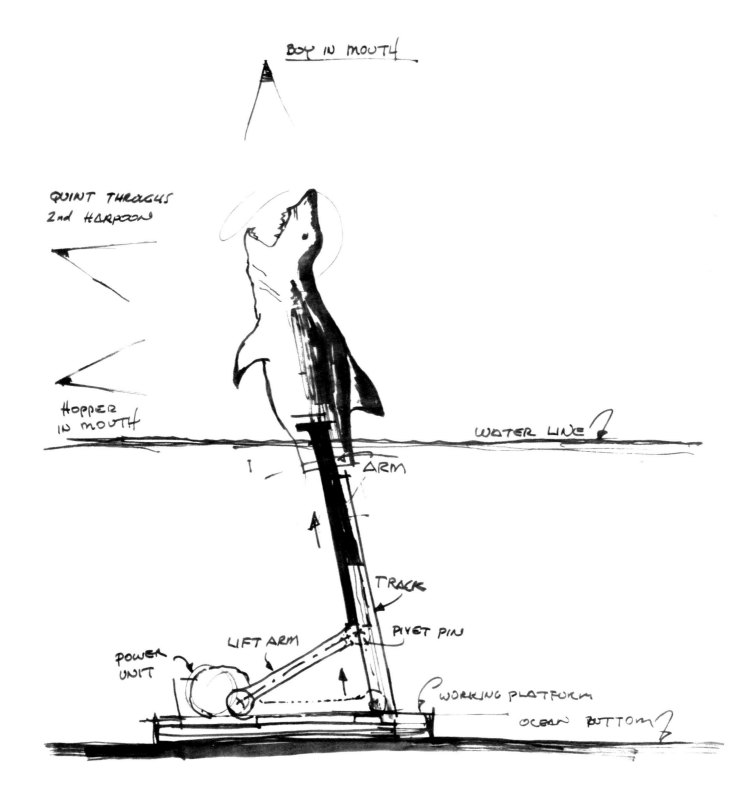

BOY IN MOUTH

QUINT THROUGH
2nd HARPOON

HOPPER
IN MOUTH

WATER LINE

ARM

TRACK

LIFT ARM

PIVET PIN

POWER
UNIT

WORKING PLATFORM

OCEAN BOTTOM

ABOVE / Joe Alves' early design sketch suggests a "half shark" for specific sequences.

ALVES OPENLY CONFERRED WITH SPIELBERG while preparing the concept drawings he had presented in Green's office. Spielberg, at the time, was clearly interested but hadn't yet officially signed on to direct *JAWS*.

"When I was preparing those drawings, Steven still wasn't signed as the director for the picture because it wasn't really a picture yet," Alves recalled, "and he wasn't yet sure that he wanted to do it at all. But I kept discussing the drawings with him to get his reactions to what I was proposing. During one of our chats he said to me, 'You know, Joe, one reason I might do this picture is just because you're so enthused about it.' I don't think I was the one who ultimately convinced him to do it, but we were having a good time working together."

Ultimately, Spielberg's attraction to the potent adventure permeating Benchley's story was the deciding factor, irresistible enough to accept the producers' offer that he direct. With some tightening of the narrative, Spielberg believed he had a real audience-grabber on his hands. That enthusiasm, matched by Alves' 'yeah, we can do this' assuredness set aloft a creative collaboration between the two men.

Following the meeting, Alves and Bill DeCinces discussed ways of making a functional shark.

"So it has to be mechanical," DeCinces agreed, "at least for some of the close up shots and when it eats people. Maybe it could be attached to a sort of pivot point at the end of the tail or something."

DeCinces took up a pencil and positioned it perpendicular below the heel of his palm. "It could pivot from the back like this, up and down and side to side," he said, moving his flattened hand around to simulate the shark's movement.

Alves agreed, thinking of how it might essentially be 'puppeteered' from below, in the water, out of view of the camera. He began sketching possible technical designs to help him envision how it might be approached and, if nothing else, as a way of convincing himself that it truly could be done.

He scribbled out several crude drawings that could be useful when shopping the idea around. It still wasn't an official production and there was no script (Benchley's book was months away from publication). But before he could even consider striking out to find someone who could make a mechanical monster, he'd have to first educate himself about real sharks.

BELOW / Joe Alves' early design sketches specify a separate "full-bodied shark" for the attack on Ben Gardner.

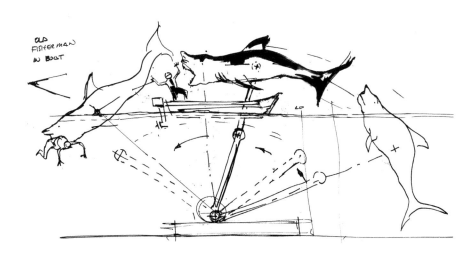

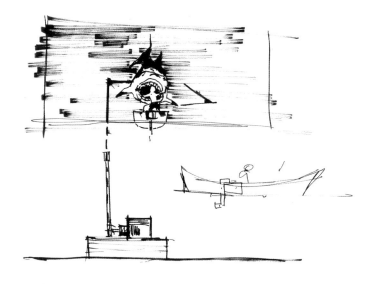

HIS FIRST STOP, THEN, was at the Scripps Institution of Oceanography in La Jolla, California. There he spoke with the staff to learn what he could about sharks, namely this *Carcharodon carcharias*, the great white shark. He learned that these fish are of prehistoric descent, they reach maturity at about the age of fifteen and, particular to the great white, they typically grow up to twenty feet in length.

Understanding more about sharks in general and some of the broad-stroke physical characteristics of the great white, it was now time to seek out an ichthyologist. Leonard Compagno, cited as a taxonomy expert who could help in the design of a believable, albeit mechanical, Hollywood shark, could be found in San Francisco at the Steinhart Aquarium of the California Academy of Sciences. It was still October of 1973 when Alves traveled to the aquarium to become the attentive pupil of Compagno, absorbing every detail of the size, shape, and physical characteristics of great white sharks. As a useful souvenir of his visit, the Aquarium loaned to Alves a massive set of great white shark jaws, those he could take back to Universal to use as a reference for accurate design and development.

BELOW / Correspondence with shark expert, Leonard Compagno.

STANFORD UNIVERSITY
STANFORD, CALIFORNIA 94305

Department of Biological Sciences
DIVISION OF SYSTEMATIC BIOLOGY

November 8, 1973

Mr. Joseph Alves
Art Director
Universal City Studios, Inc.
100 Universal City Plaza
Universal City, California 91608

Dear Joe

According to a regression analysis line that I computed for tooth size vs. total length in the great white shark, the set of jaws from the California Academy of Sciences that you have came from a shark about 4 meters or 13.1 feet long.

I'm still most uncertain as to what would be a fair consultant fee for my services. Various people that I asked about this suggested that about $100.00 would be adequate for the time last Tuesday. If this is exorbitant please let me know.

It was very nice to meet you. I hope I can be of further service. Unfortunately a fresh shark has not been collected at the time of writing this letter.

Sincerely yours

Leonard Compagno

November 15, 1973

Mr. Leonard Compagno
Division of Systematic Biology
Department of Biological Sciences
Stanford University
Stanford, CA   94305

Dear Leonard:

Thank you for your services in determining the size of the shark based on the jaws. It will be a great help to me.

The Production Department feels that $100.00 would be fine on a daily basis. If a more extensive period of time is needed, we would make other arrangements. It seems the normal rate in the past for technical advise has been $350.00 on a weekly basis.

I am sure I will require your help again. At that time we could fly you down at our expense, or I could come up and meet with you. If an extended period of your time is needed, I would give you ample notice so we could make the proper arrangements.

Please send us your Social Security number so we can expedite payment of your $100.00. It is the policy of our Accounting Department that the Social Security Number be noted on all payments made to individuals.

Once again let me express my thanks for your services and the pleasant afternoon I spent at the Academy.

Very truly yours,

Joe Alves
Art Director

JA:db1

From his research, Alves became intimately knowledgeable about great white sharks which, coupled with his film design sensibilities, helped him determine a size and shape that would best suit the 'character' of the beast.

"I made a large profile drawing of the shark I had in mind, then used that to guide me in sculpting a four-foot relief model. Essentially, it was based on the profile of real sharks that measured about twelve-and-a-half feet long. In my research and through the guidance of Leonard Compagno, I noticed that as the sharks grew to about fifteen feet long or more, they got sort of 'girthy' – they had a lot more girth to them, and I didn't want a shark that looked fat; from a design sensibility, I wanted a sleeker shark that looked to be a more formidable opponent yet would still be considered accurate."

Alves and Spielberg discussed the size of this monster shark, both agreeing that a twenty-five-foot specimen – twice the size of a twelve-and-a-half-foot great white but retaining its body size and contours – would be the best length to settle on, all the while both knowing that, in order to get what they wanted, they'd be best served if they provided two proposed sizes for executive approval: one at twenty feet and another a thirty feet. If the executives settled on twenty-five, as the two anticipated they would, then the executives would believe it was *their* decision, *their* idea, and thus, getting *them* invested in the effort to build this shark.

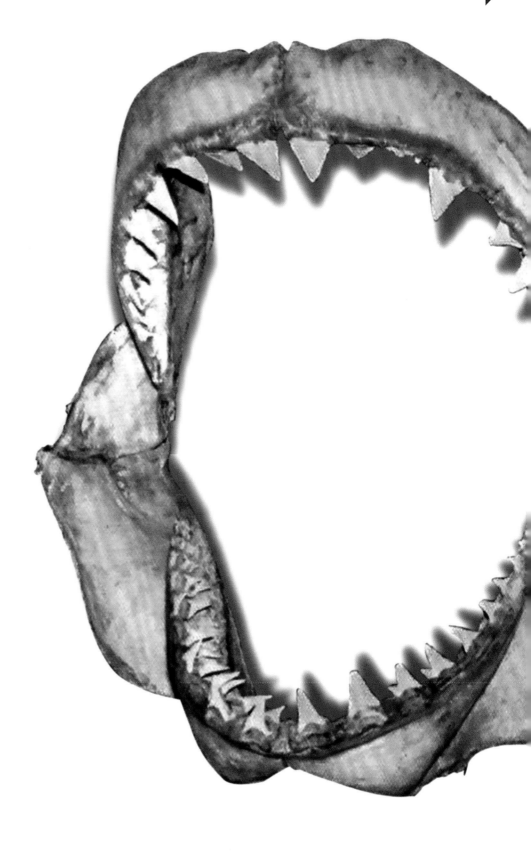

RIGHT / Great white shark jaws loaned from the Steinhart Aquarium (later used in filming the *Orca*'s departure to hunt the shark).

Alves tapped Universal art department illustrator, John Datu Arensma, to make two full-size profile drawings, one of a twenty-foot shark and another of a thirty-foot shark.

With the full-size drawings pasted on the walls of the Universal parking garage, Alves and Spielberg collected the executives so they could make their decision. All agreed that the twenty-footer wasn't quite big enough but the thirty-footer was simply horrendous. "Maybe something in between these two," they wondered.

"Oh – like twenty-five feet? That would be good," Alves offered.

"Yes, Joe. Twenty-five feet would be best."

"Ok, sure. We'll do that. Thank you."

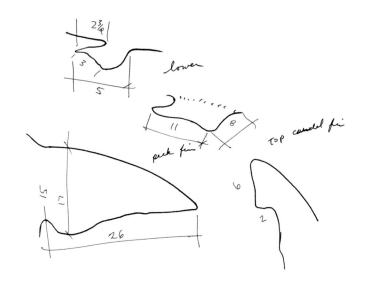

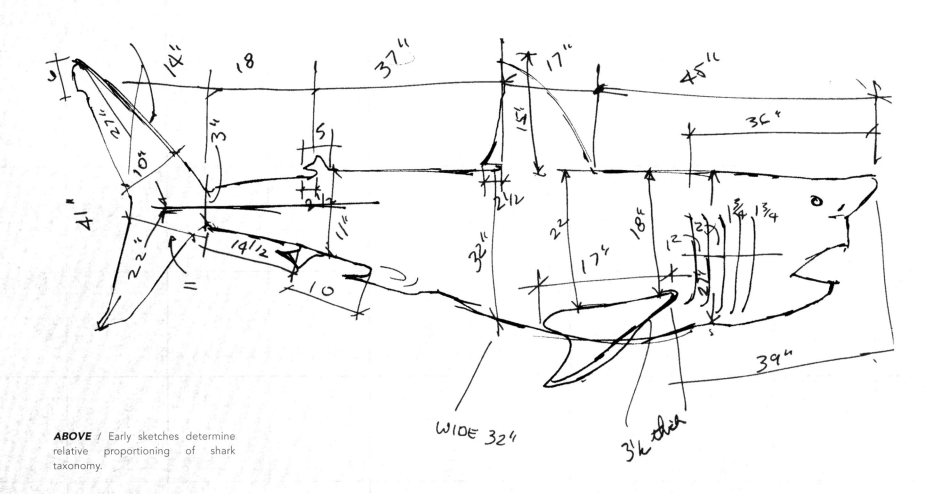

ABOVE / Early sketches determine relative proportioning of shark taxonomy.

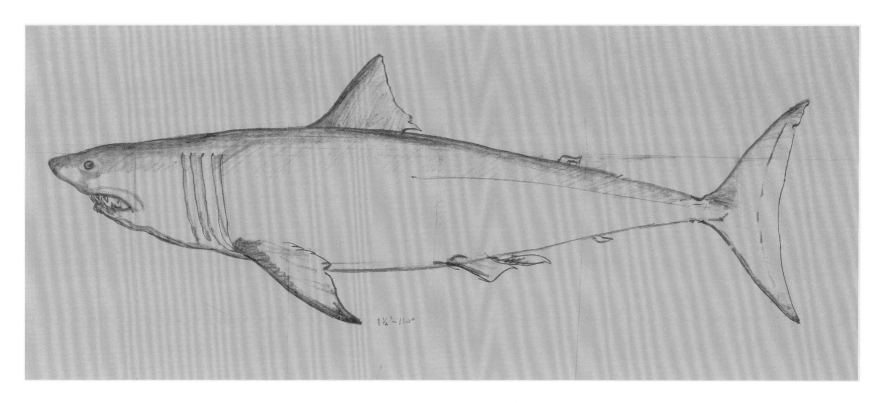

ABOVE / Joe Alves' initial shark profile sketch to guide in creation of a relief sculpture.

ABOVE / Joe Alves' four-foot relief sculpture to be used as the design pattern for the full-sized shark.

IN THE MEANTIME, Alves had begun his search for an individual or a team that could help construct a functional mechanical shark. He first visited the Walt Disney Studios. They loved the idea but wouldn't agree to take it on location to operate for filming, so that turned out to be a non-starter. Next, he met with effects expert Joe Lombardi (television's *Star Trek*, *The Godfather*), who also appreciated the challenge but warned it would take over a year to deliver and, even then, there would be no way to operate it in a real ocean; it would only work in a studio tank.

With growing concern, Alves pondered that he might be defeated in his quest. Pushing back despair, he remembered one other name mentioned by a Disney sculptor, Jim Kasey, who suggested: "You might give Bob Mattey a call."

Who?

Born in New Jersey in 1910, Robert A. Mattey got his first taste of movie magic at the age of sixteen when he accompanied his father, Robert Sr., to Hollywood to fashion the unique coins as well as some effects miniatures for Cecil B. DeMille's 1927 biblical epic, *The King of Kings*. Bob Jr. was instantly awed by the creativity of the movie-making process, especially the sets and props. He determined, at that moment, that he'd find his way into the film effects business.

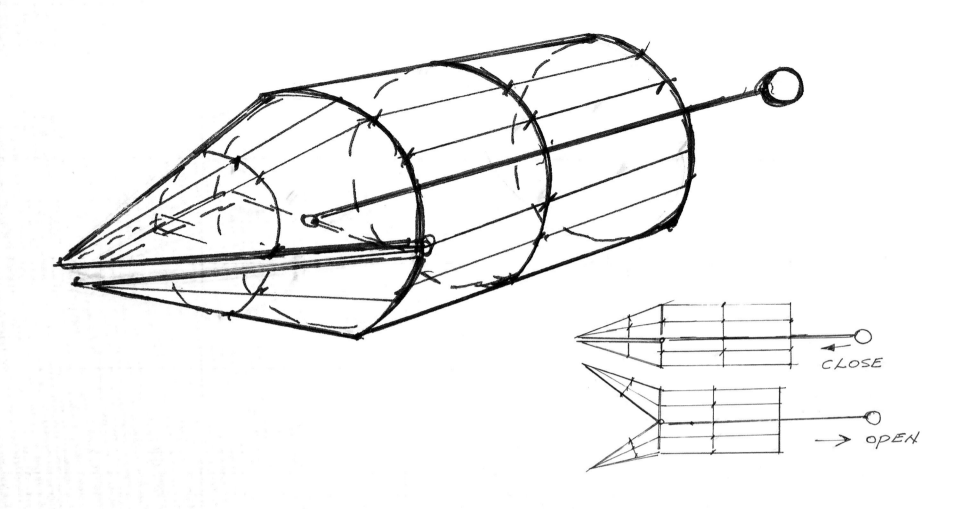

CLOSE

OPEN

He would soon tally an impressive list of effects achievements that spanned the likes of 1933's *King Kong*, 1934's *Tarzan and His Mate*, and 1936's wildly popular serial, *Flash Gordon*. It was his development of a believable giant octopus for Republic Pictures' *Wake of the Red Witch* that gained Mattey the attention of Walt Disney Studios; they needed a giant squid for the upcoming *20,000 Leagues Under the Sea*. That assignment would begin Mattey's two-decade relationship with Disney Studios, working mechanical effects for both film as well as theme park creations (the hippos of the Jungle Ride, for example).

When Alves came looking for the reportedly retired Mattey to solve a shark problem, the affable effects wizard effused, "Sure, we can do that – we can do anything! How about I start with a sort of wire frame," Mattey offered, "to show how we can make the head move side to side and make the jaws open and close? If that's good, we'll continue on from there, OK?"

OK, Alves thought. *This guy seems like he can pull it off.*

After demonstrating Mattey's wire-frame shark head with working jaws to Richard Zanuck, the producer urged, "So, if Bob's ready to work on this, I guess it's time for you to find us a place to shoot this, right?" Almost.

ALVES KNEW THAT, before he went anywhere, Mattey needed a crack team to help him build the shark. Mattey, however, had already been thinking this next step through, culling his own list of capable candidates to make up the effects team. It was an off-the-lot endeavor so both men had freedom to pick and choose as they pleased.

The first name on Mattey's list was a fellow in the Universal effects department named Roy Arbogast. The word on Arbogast was that he knew a lot about plastics and foams and the science behind them; he might be the best guy to help develop the skin of this beast. And, upon paying a visit to Universal's plastics shop – usually referred to as the Rubber Room – the two found Arbogast busy making breakaway bottles. Alves and Mattey explained their need for a shark skin. Arbogast took it all in with an unexpected calm, later revealing that he'd been anticipating their visit.

Some weeks prior, Arbogast had been called aside by Dave Lopez, a mentor of his in the Universal effects shop, who escorted him to the studio parking garage to show him the two large-scale shark drawings. "They say they want this thing to work in the ocean," Lopez scoffed. Arbogast was intrigued; he thought it could be an interesting project.

Now standing with Alves and Mattey, Arbogast began a dissertation regarding the technical properties of various foams and urethanes that he had worked with in the past and how they might work for the shark. "Urethane is probably best to start with," Arbogast suggested, "and we'll need to decide on the best shore for it – that's the hardness and memory rating of the rubber. And it needs to be water repellent so it won't just soak it up like a sponge, right? And you'll probably need some plastics or rubber for eyes and teeth, too." The three discussed what the 'neutral position' of the shark's mouth should be, as molded. If molded in a closed position, the rubber would likely tear when the mouth opens full. If molded too far open, though, the rubber would unrealistically buckle and bulge when the mouth would close. And as Arbogast went on about this and other various details and considerations over which he clearly commanded an encyclopedic precision, Alves and Mattey agreed: he's on the team.

Next on Mattey's list was Ritchie Helmer, a young guy who was handy with electronic switches and such. There was also Tim Baar, an experienced effects technician who had won an Academy Award for his work on George Pal's *The Time Machine* (1960).

BOTTOM LEFT / Roy Arbogast.

BOTTOM RIGHT / Sketch indicating neutral mouth position and jaw hinge placement.

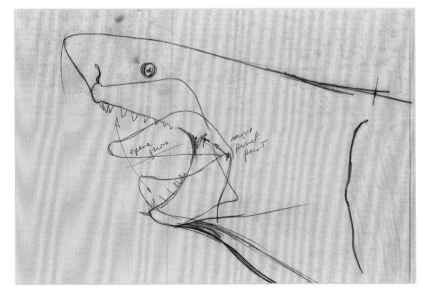

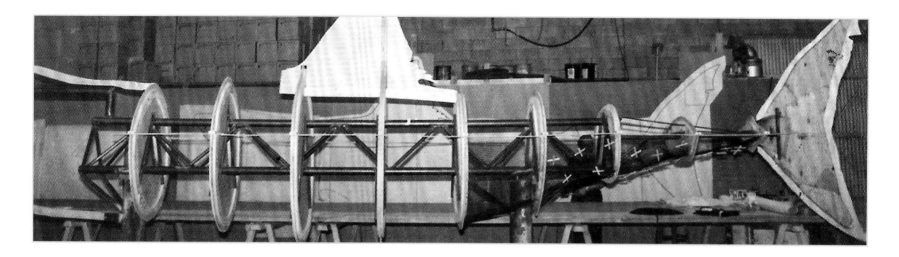

He was also a long-time friend of Mattey's so he was on the team, too. Next came the Wood brothers, Gary and Mike; they were respected for their talents in welding. Get them on the team. Conrad 'Whitey' Krumm was known for his work in mechanical sleds, exactly what the shark would need to glide forward and back. He should be on the team. Stan Mahoney was recognized as a craftsman with useful lathe skills, perfect for fabricating the various rams, rods, and actuators that would make up much of the mechanical shark's innards. OK – get him, too.

What this team now needed was a place to secretly build the mechanical monster. Mattey, a resident of Sunland, CA, checked in with Rolly Harper's Catering and Motion Picture Rentals business in nearby Sun Valley. They had a huge open warehouse, easy to get to, and, luckily, available to rent. The team had a home. They started setting up shop right away, assembling the gear and arranging work areas within the giant single-room warehouse. Surveying the seven guys as they readied to take on the most complex effect ever conceived, Alves mused to himself:

Look at that... 'The Magnificent Seven.' Let's find out.

ABOVE / Work on full-size shark frame for sculpting outer body.

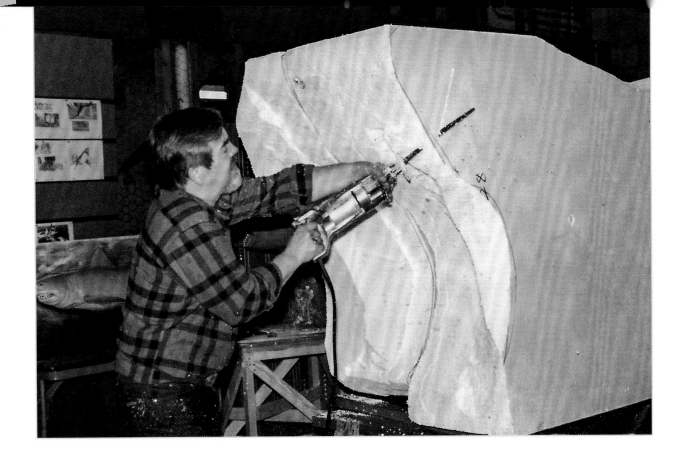

LEFT / Sculptor Don Chandler at work (note Joe Alves' relief model at far left).

BELOW / Don Chandler's shark sculpt in progress.

ABOVE / Constructing the shark,
inside out and outside in.

Before setting off to scout locations to serve as the fictitious Amity Island, Joe secured engineer and technical draftsman Frank Wurmser to render technical specifications as required by Mattey and from which his Magnificent Seven would work. He also handed over his four-foot shark sculpture to Don Chandler, the sculptor who had rendered a collection of life-sized frightening figures for *Scream, Pretty Peggy*, a made-for-television movie for which Alves served as art director.

Alves turned Chandler loose to render a full-sized – that is, the full twenty-five feet in length – clay model of the shark from which an exterior mold could be made, the mold that Arbogast would use

to pour and pull the shark's skin. And, to keep the shark looking as realistic as possible, Alves secured the ongoing oversight of Leonard Compagno, signed on as a consultant in November 1973.

Since Universal was hoping to release the film quickly in association with the publication of the novel (they hoped to cash in on the film before the book ultimately tanked), the shark would be constructed concurrently from the inside out and the outside in.

Don Chandler was responsible for matching Alves' sculpted design while Roy Arbogast was responsible for ensuring that Mattey's mechanisms would fit properly within Chandler's sculpt.

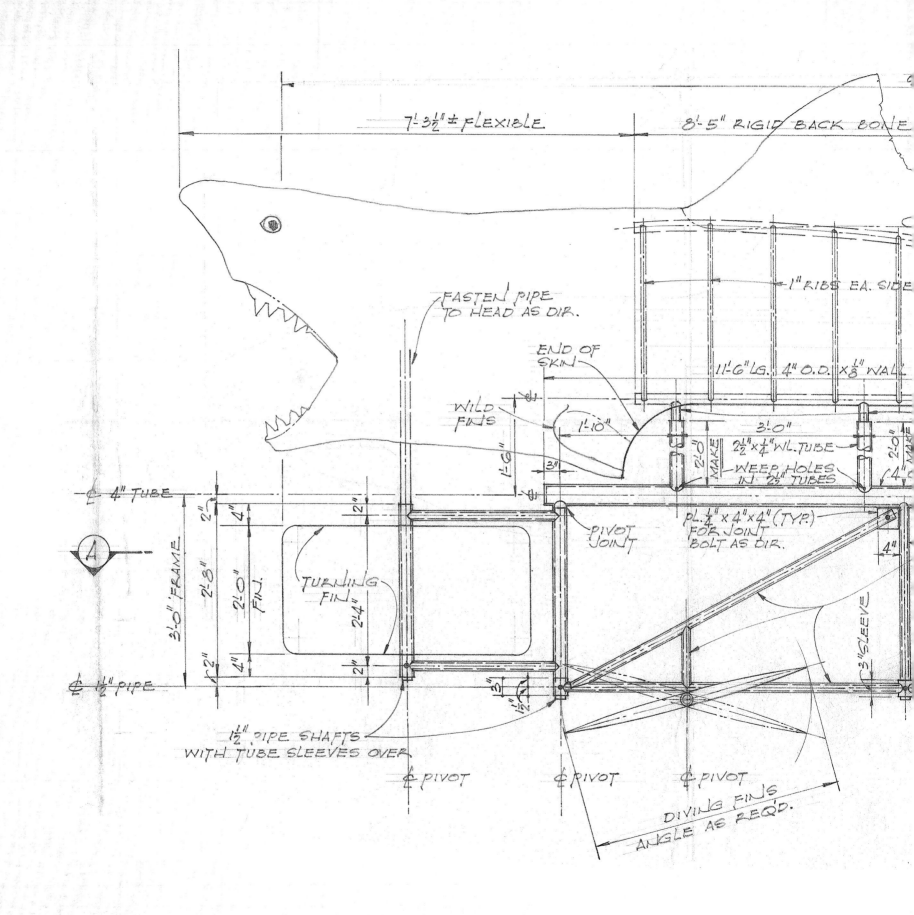

7'-3½"± FLEXIBLE

8'-5" RIGID BACK BONE

FASTEN PIPE
TO HEAD AS DIR.

END OF
SKIN

1" RIBS EA. SIDE

11'-6" LG. 4" O.D. × ⅛" WALL

WILD
FINS

1'-10"

1'-6"

3"

3'-0"
2½" × ¼" WL. TUBE

WEEP HOLES
IN 2½" TUBES

2'-0"
MAKE

2'-0"
MAKE

4"

¢ 4" TUBE

2"

4"

2"

PIVOT
JOINT

PL. ¼" × 4" × 4" (TYP.)
FOR JOINT
BOLT AS DIR.

4"

4"

A

3'-0" FRAME

2'-8"

2'-0"
FIN.

2'-4"

TURNING
FIN

3" SLEEVE

¢ 1½" PIPE

2"

4"

2"

3"

½"

1½" PIPE SHAFTS
WITH TUBE SLEEVES OVER

¢ PIVOT

¢ PIVOT

¢ PIVOT

DIVING FINS
ANGLE AS REQ'D.

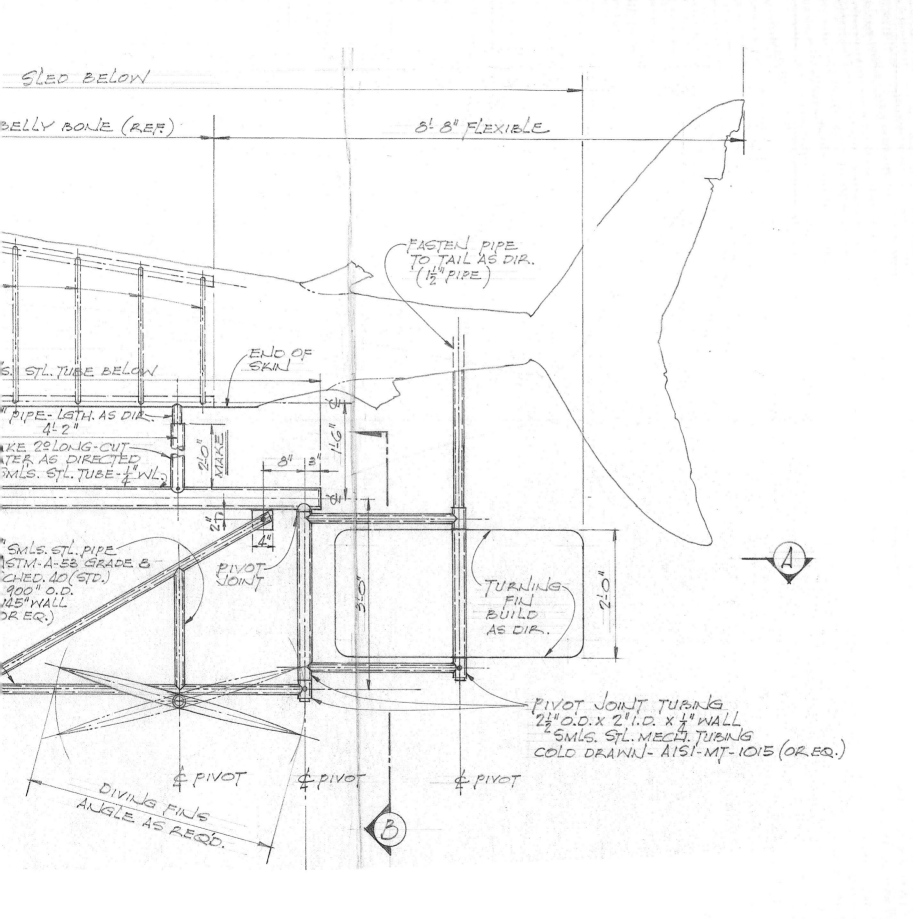

SLED BELOW

BELLY BONE (REF.)

8'-8" FLEXIBLE

FASTEN PIPE
TO TAIL AS DIR.
(1½" PIPE)

END OF
SKIN

S. STL. TUBE BELOW

" PIPE- LGTH. AS DIR.
4'-2"
KE 2° LONG-CUT
TER AS DIRECTED
SMLS. STL. TUBE-¼"WL.

MAKE
2'-0"

8"   3"

1'-6"

2"

4"

" SMLS. STL. PIPE
STM-A-53 GRADE B
CHED. 40 (STD.)
900" O.D.
145" WALL
OR EQ.)

PIVOT
JOINT

3'-0"

TURNING
FIN
BUILD
AS DIR.

2'-0"

⟨A⟩

PIVOT JOINT TUBING
2½" O.D. x 2" I.D. x ¼" WALL
SMLS. STL. MECH. TUBING
COLD DRAWN- AISI-MT-1015 (OR EQ.)

₡ PIVOT   ₡ PIVOT   ₡ PIVOT

DIVING FINS
ANGLE AS REQ'D.

⟨B⟩

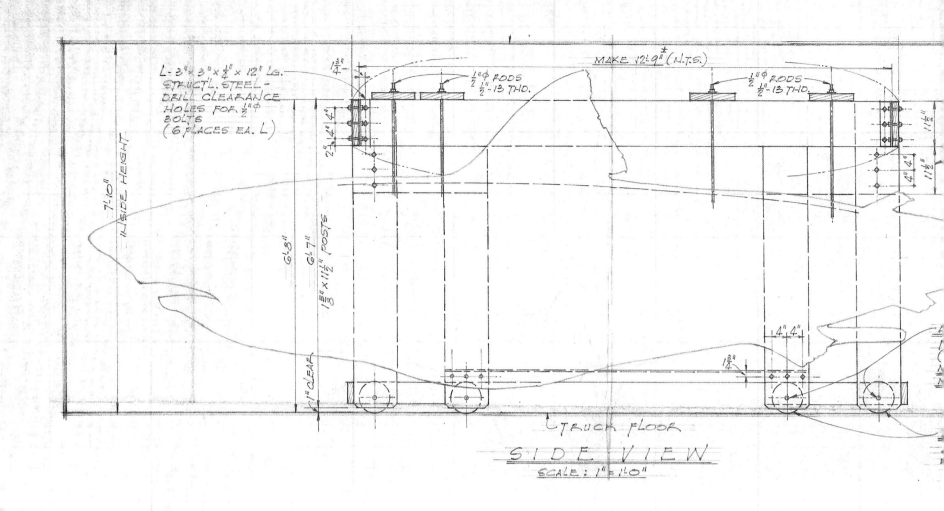

L-3"×3"×¼"×12" LG.
STRUCT'L. STEEL -
DRILL CLEARANCE
HOLES FOR ½"Φ
BOLTS
(6 PLACES EA. L)

1¾"

MAKE 12'-9"± (N.T.S.)

½"Φ RODS
½"-13 THD.

½"Φ RODS
½"-13 THD.

2¼"×4"

4" 4"

1½"

INSIDE HEIGHT

7'-10"

6'-8"

6'-7"

1⅝"×11½" POSTS

1" CLEAR.

4" 4"

1¾"

TRUCK FLOOR

SIDE VIEW

SCALE: 1"=1'-0"

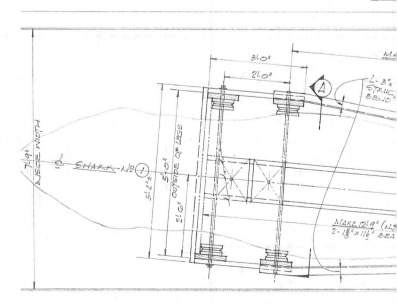

3'-0"

2'-0"

INSIDE WIDTH

7'-0"

5'-4¼"

SHARK N° ①

5'-0" OUTSIDE OF LEGS

2'-6"

L-3"
STRUCT'L
BEND

MAKE 12'-9" (N.T.
2-1⅝"×11½" EA.

A

THIS SPREAD / Frank Wurmser's technical
drawing specifies shark transport system.

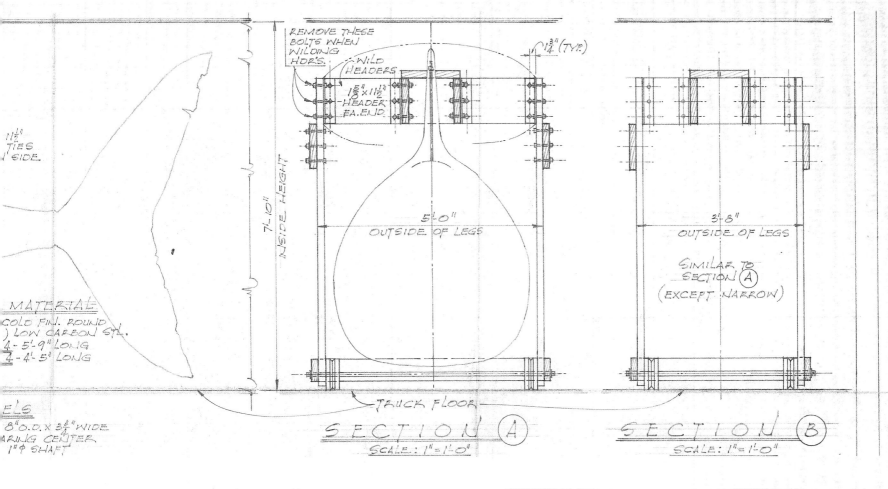

SECTION (A)

SCALE: 1"=1'-0"

SECTION (B)

SCALE: 1"=1'-0"

REMOVE THESE
BOLTS WHEN
WILDING
HDR'S.

WILD
HEADERS

1 5/8" x 11 1/2"
HEADER
EA. END.

1 3/4" (TYP.)

5'-0"
OUTSIDE OF LEGS

3'-8"
OUTSIDE OF LEGS

SIMILAR TO
SECTION (A)
(EXCEPT NARROW)

7'-10"
INSIDE HEIGHT

TRUCK FLOOR

MATERIAL

COLD FIN. ROUND
LOW CARBON STL.
4 - 5'-9" LONG
4 - 4'-5" LONG

8" O.D. X 3 3/4" WIDE
BEARING CENTER
1" ∅ SHAFT

1 1/2"
TIES
SIDE.

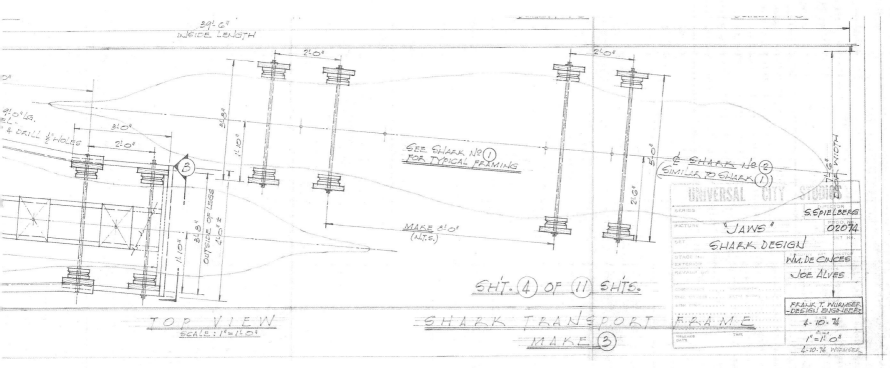

TOP VIEW

SCALE: 1"=1'-0"

SHARK TRANSPORT FRAME

MAKE (3)

39'-6"
INSIDE LENGTH

2'-0"

2'-0"

SEE SHARK No (1)
FOR TYPICAL FRAMING

₵ SHARK No (2)
(SIMILAR TO SHARK (1))

MAKE 8'-0"
(N.T.S.)

SHT. (4) OF (11) SHTS.

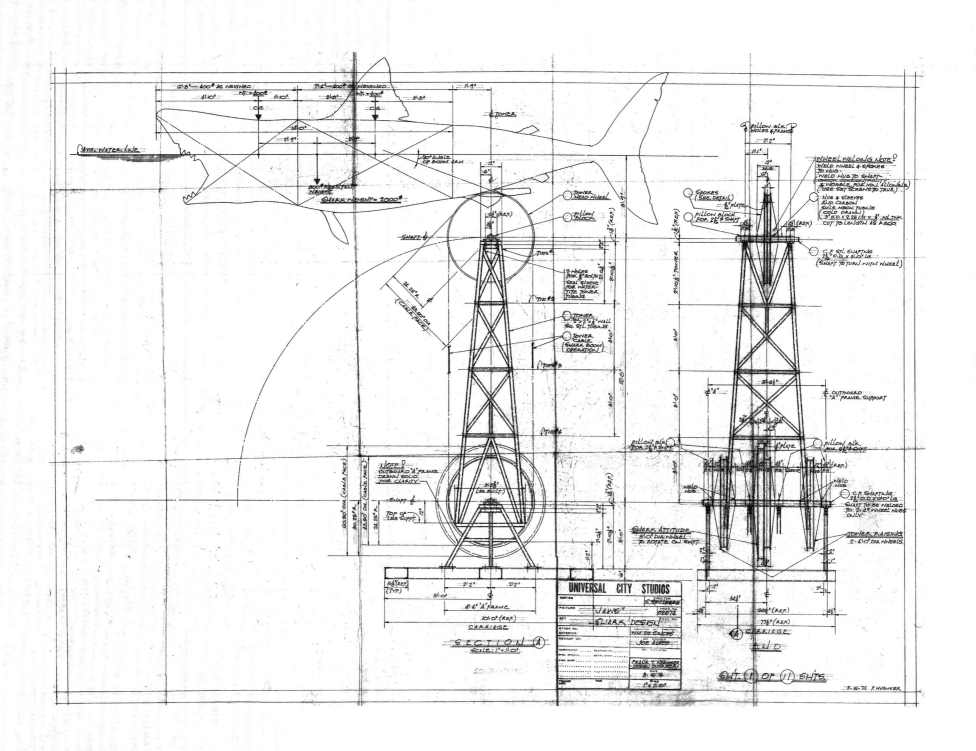

UNIVERSAL CITY STUDIOS

PICTURE "JAWS"

SET SHARK DESIGN

Bob Mattey had conceived an elaborate crane-arm-and-gimbal platform that would rest on the ocean bottom, controlled from a remote rig, allowing him and his team to make the shark perform to director Spielberg's every desire. And, in order to capture the action that Benchley had described in his novel as well as in his initial screenplay draft, it became clear to Mattey and Alves that there would need to be several sharks constructed.

To account for the presence of protruding hoses, harnesses, and cables, those that would need to be hidden from the camera's view, there would be three sharks built. First would be a 'platform shark' that would be fully articulated for movement (head shaking and biting) and would be attached to the submersible platform with the crane-arm-and-gimbal mechanism. There would also be two 'swimming sharks' – a left-to-right shark (for filming the left-hand side profile) and a right-to-left shark (for filming the right-hand side profile).

Of course, with each shark estimated to weigh in at 2,000 pounds, transport would be an equally vexing matter. As such, Mattey worked with Frank Wurmser to specify a frame-and-harness solution to safely move the sharks and all attending contraptions from the Sunland warehouse in California to... well, to wherever the ultimate filming location would be.

And so all was progressing well. Publisher Doubleday was still prepping Benchley's novel for an early 1974 release. Director Spielberg was reviewing Benchley's draft script (and revisions), and producers Zanuck and Brown were remaining attentive and supportive of the effort, all the while preparing their feature-in-the-wings, *The Sting*, for a December release

And so it seemed long, long ago, during the presentation in Marshall Green's office, that the *JAWS* project might never get afloat. But, in the course of a couple months' time, the behind-the-scenes players had been brought together, the details of the monstrous shark had been laid out, and work was underway. The *JAWS* project was given a charge number – it was officially in pre-production. And, with that, Alves confirmed to Zanuck and Brown that, indeed, it was time to break down the working script and begin scouting locations where all hell would break loose.

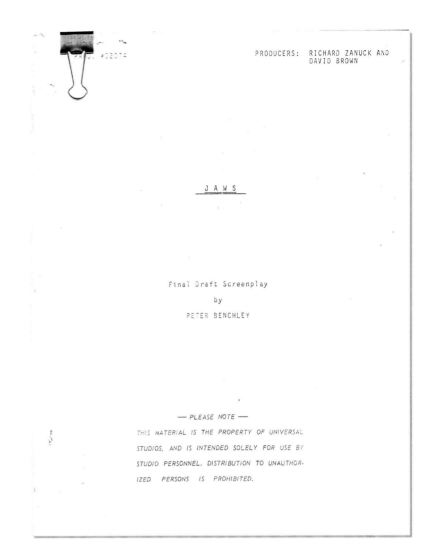

PRODUCERS: RICHARD ZANUCK AND
DAVID BROWN

J A W S

Final Draft Screenplay
by
PETER BENCHLEY

— PLEASE NOTE —
THIS MATERIAL IS THE PROPERTY OF UNIVERSAL
STUDIOS, AND IS INTENDED SOLELY FOR USE BY
STUDIO PERSONNEL. DISTRIBUTION TO UNAUTHOR-
IZED PERSONS IS PROHIBITED.

THIS SPREAD / Frank Wurmser's detailed drawing of Bob Mattey's crane-and-arm mechanism.

EARLY BREAKDOWN

THE FIRST RECORDED BREAKDOWN attributed to *JAWS* was in no way related to mechanical malfunctions nor human frailty – it was the script. Specifically, it was production designer Joe Alves' exercise of interpreting the shooting script and 'breaking it down' into production and design elements.

Benchley approached scriptwriting as any novelist might; he'd begin by transposing his original narrative into a screenplay. Spielberg, already skilled in screen-friendly storytelling, wanted heightened excitement, faster pacing, and more compelling characters. The two conferred on a couple of iterations, Benchley confident in his novelist's approach, Spielberg, alternately, convinced in his own show-don't-tell and less-is-more filmmaking sensibility. In the mix, Joe Alves was eager to begin his location scouting but first needed a script to breakdown as a to guide his explorations.

"Before I set out in December 1973 to scout the picture, I first needed a script to break down. In late November, then, I worked from Benchley's second draft of the script. I knew it wasn't complete but I needed to get started in defining what the production would need as far as locations and overall design elements."

Oftentimes, while performing the breakdown, a production designer begins making design decisions based on what *isn't* specified by the script.

"If the script calls out a public beach where some action is taking place, and this is a tourist-y sort of situation, then I'd want to probably include a bandstand, a boardwalk, cabanas, and those sorts of things that provide a festive setting.

"But what's really interesting is the progression you see in this process: the script indicates how a scene will play, then the script breakdown further refines and sometimes changes some of that, then the director's own interpretation ultimately delivers the final result.

"For example, in the opening scene with Chrissie, Benchley described a house on the beach where a young girl and guy come out to take a swim; for that I'm breaking down that I need to provide a house on or by the beach for the director to shoot. But since the guy was drunk and ends up passing out as Chrissie is attacked and killed by the shark, Steven decided a beach party with a bonfire would be a better idea since it gives a stronger reason why the guy would be drunk and then pass out while the girl swims away in the nighttime water. We all agreed that was a better approach, and that's how that particular scene evolved from the original script treatment. And so, for that, I made an adjustment to my original set list and design to stage the beach party. And, in the end, it's a better-executed scene that works really well to set the tone for the rest of the film."

As it would turn out, *JAWS* would be fluid in its design and execution. Alves would make additional script breakdown notes as script revisions were provided to him. By the end, two scripts would be written by Benchley, modifications would be provided by Steven Spielberg, and even an uncredited rewrite by celebrated playwright Howard Sackler was incorporated, all of that before veteran writer Carl Gottlieb would be brought aboard to provide key revisions while alternately performing in front of the camera as Amity's own news journalist, Harry Meadows. And with the stream of revisions, Alves would continue to enhance his breakdown notes, even to the extent that he'd employ some shorthand by way of quick sketches that would be precursor to a collection of storyboards he'd soon render.

LEFT / Joe Alves' original breakdown notes, written on the pages of a 9" x 12" legal pad, based on Peter Benchley's script.

FORM NUMBER GEN. 5

(GIRL TAKEN UNDERWATER)
LARGE HUMP IN WATER
NEEDED

SC. 1 · EXT. SOUTH SHORE OF LONG ISLAND (4)

(WHAT ABOUT UNDERWATER
SHOTS FOR INTRO?)
— MOONLIT NIGHT · WINDLESS · MID JUNE —
SHOT FR. 200 YDS. OFF SHORE LOOKING
AT WHITE SAND BEACH · LOW DUNES ·
EXPENSIVE HOUSE IN BACKGROUND —
MOVE IN ON ONE HOUSE W/ LIGHTS ON
GIRL & GUY COME OUT ONTO PORCH THEN RUN
DOWN BEACH.

SC. 2 · EXT. BEACH (N)
GIRL & GUY PLAYING AROUND — SHE GOES IN
WATER, HE FALLS ASLEEP.

SC. 3 · EXT. OFFSHORE (N)
50 YDS OFFSHORE — CHRISTINE SWIMMING AWAY
FR. BEACH — WATER IS VERY CALM. — CAMERA
PANS — WE SEE LARGE SHAPE IN WATER —
IT MOVE TOWARD CHRIS.

SC. 4 · EXT. OFFSHORE (N)
CHRIS · AWARE SOMETHING WRONG — SHAPE COME
CLOSE TO HER. WAVE PRESSURE LIFTS HER UP.
SHE STARTS TO SHORE — SOMETHING JERKS
HER DOWN — SHE REACHES DOWN TO
HER FOOT — SCREAMS — THE SHAPE COMES
AGAIN — PULLS HER DOWN — A FEW
WAVELETS — THEN THE WATER IS CALM.

SC 7 BRODY & CASSIDY — HEAR LEONARD WHISTLE — RUN
TO THE OTHER END OF BEACH — LEONARD · RETCH'G
IN SAND.
SC 8 TANGLED SKEIN OF WEED & KELP — LITTLE REMAINS
OF CHRISTINE — HEAD · GREY FACE · SHOULDER · ONE BREAST.
SC 9 BRODY TURNS AWAY
SC 10 BRODY HAS CASSIDY IDENTIFY CHRIST'S BODY
THEY ALL VOMIT.
SC 11 EXT. PUBLIC · BEACH PARKING LOT (D)
PARKING LOT JUST BEHIND DUNES. EMPTY.
POLICE CAR TURNS OFF PATH ONTO LOT.
DIRT LOT. STOPS AT ENTRANCE TO PATH LEAD'G
TO BEACH. BRODY GETS OUT GOES TO TRUCK
TAKE OUT SIGNS "NO SWIMMING"
"NO SWIMMING BY ORDER OF AMITY P.D."
ANOTHER CAR SPEEDS INTO THE LOT — VAUGHAN
& MEADOWS GET OUT. THEY TALK — BRODY
MOVES OFF UP THE PATH · DISAPPEARS OVER DUNES

SC 12 INT. POLICE STATION (D)
BRODY SITTING IN HIS OFFICE DOING PAPER-
WORK — GETS A CALL

SC 13 EXT. OCEAN (D)
BRODY & HENDRICKS LEAVING HARBOR
19² OUTBOARD — HENDRICKS DRIVE LEAVES
THE HARBOR MOUTH — PUSHES THROTTLE FORWARD
BOAT BEGINS TO PLANE.

SC 14 BOSTON WHALER 2 BOYS ABOARD —
CHUM'G — CLOTHESLINE HANG'G OVERBOARD · AT BOW
— BOY HAUL IN LINE BIG SHARKS HOOK — DUCK HEAD
— BRODY TELLS THEM TO MOVE ON.

SC 16 EXT. PRIVATE BEACH (D)
SMALL CROWD ON BEACH — MAN ARGUES W/
POLICEMAN — "NO SWIMMING" SIGNS IN BACKGROUND.

SC 17 EXT. MAIN STREET EVENING
ABOUT 7:30 – 8:00 AT NIGHT. STREET ALMOST
EMPTY — MOST STORE CLOSED — HALF WAY DO.
ST. WE SEE LIGHT FR. WINDOW OF BOUTIQUE.
CAMERA MOVES DO. ST. STOP OUTSIDE
BOUTIQUE CALLED "BIBELOT". WINDOW FULL
OUT CHIC N'CKS · NAVAHO JEWELRY ETC. WE SEE
MAN & WOMAN APPROACHING WINDOW FR. INSIDE.
— THEY PULL OUT SHARK'S TEETH JEWELRY —
HE STABS HER IN THE BUTT W/ ONE.
SIGN READS "AUTHENTIC SHARKS-TOOTH JEWELRY"

SC 18 EXT. ORIENT POINT · FERRY DOCK (D)
CARS STREAM'G OFF FERRY — DUSTY PICK-UP
— SIGN ON TRUCK — "WOODS HOLE OCEANOGRAPHIC
INSTITUTE" — BACK OF TRUCK FULL OF · STUFF
ALUM. CAGE · SCUBA TANKS · ETC. — TRUCK MOVE
AWAY FROM DOCK ALONG ROAD.

SC 19 INT. PICKUP TRUCK (D)
MATT HOOPER · AT WHEEL · DISHEVELED — COME
TO INTERSECTION — SIGN POINTS LEFT TO "GREENPORT-
SHELTER ISLAND, AMITY, HAMPTONS. HOOPER
CHECKS MAP — PUTS FINGER ON AMITY — TURNS OFF.

SC 20 EXT. ABELARD ARMS HOTEL (D)
A RELIC OF AMITY'S MORE GRACIOUS DAYS — WOODEN
MANSE · HUGE · RAMBLING · VICTORIAN · OLD CLIENTELE
ONLY HOTEL IN TOWN? — OLD PACKARDS

LIMO. PULLS UP — DOORMAN TAKES OLD WOMAN'S
HAND. HE AS DECREPIT AS SHE · HELPS HER UP
STEPS — CHAUFFEUR · DRIVES PACKARD OFF TO
AREA MARKED "PARKING"
MOMENT LATER — PICKUP COME INTO DRIVEWAY
— STOPS — THEN MOVES TO PARKING LOT.

SC 21 INT ABELARD ARMS LOBBY (D)
LOBBY · OLD · VICTORIAN OVER STUFF
FURNITURE · CHANDELIERS · OLD PEOPLE SIT'G
AROUND · DESK CLERK CHECK'G IN PEOPLE
FR. PACKARD · BELL BOY HELPS THEM TO ELEVATOR.
— SILENCE OF LOBBY BROKEN · BY HOOPERS
CLANG'G OF SCUBA EQUIP · CLERK REG. SHOCK.
SC 22 P.O.V. HOOPER STRIDING ACROSS LOBBY
W/ GEAR. EVERYONE LOOK'G.
HOOPER TALKS W/ CLERK — BELL BOY HELPS
HOOPER W/ GEAR. THEY MOVE TO ELEVATOR.

SC 23 INT. ROOM 206 (D)
HOOPER'S ROOM · LARGE · CHINTZY · ANTI-MAC-
ASSARS COVER THE BACK OF 2 STUFFED CHAIRS
— 3/4 BED CANOPIED — LAMPS W/ FLORAL PATTERN
GLASS SHADES — HOOPER & BELLBOY — GIVES HIM TIP.

SC 24 INT. BATHROOM · RM 206
HOOPER TURNS ON SHOWER — TEST'G WATER
W/ HIS HANDS. GO TO SINK — LOOK'G IN MIRROR
SOMETHING IN HIS TEETH. GRABS LIGHT · BARE
BULB — GETS SHOCK — KNOCKED ACROSS ROOM.
INTO SHOWER.

SC 25 EXT. DOCK AMITY (HARBOR DOWN)
AMITY HARBOR IS QUIET · A FLOCK OF TERNS
WHEEL OVER SOME SOLITARY · CAWING OF A FEW
SEAGULLS — 12 OR SO BOATS IN THEIR SLIPS
SMALL SHACK AT THE END OF THE PIER · SIGN ON IT
"HARBORMASTER" · HOOPER GETS OUT OF TRUCK TO SHACK.

SC 26 EXT. INT. HARBOR MASTERS SHACK (D)
HOOPER APPROACHES SHACK · TALK TO HARBOR
MASTER ABOUT RENT'G A BOAT — PAYS $25
— WE PAN TO THE BOAT · HOLD AT A SCRUFFY
OLD BOAT · CHIPPING POINT ETC. — HOOPER
GOES TO BOAT. — HARBORMASTER · CALLS
BRODY ON PHONE

SC 27 EXT DOCK (D)
BRODY'S CAR PARKED ON END OF DOCK
HE STANDS BY WAITING FOR HOOPERS BOAT
TO COME IN — 2 OTHER BOAT ENTER HARBOR
BRODY WATCHES THEM — THEN HE SEE HOOPERS
BOAT ROUND THE POINT — ENTER HARBOR &
THE DOCK

SC 28 BRODY SMALL FIGURE AT END OF PIER · WATCH'G
HOOPER TIE UP BOAT. BRODY SEEM IMPRESS
W/ ALL HOOPERS GEAR. THEY TALK. — HOOPER
TAKE OFF WET SUIT BRODY SEES SCARS MADE
BY SHARKS ON HOOPER'S BODY

SC 29 INT POLICE STATION (D)
BRODY SITTING IN HIS OFFICE — SMALLISH
NONDESCRIPT RM — FURNISHED W/ NORMAL THINGS
HE TALK INTO INTERCOM. — VAUGHAN · ENTERS
FOLLOWED BY MEADOWS & HOOPER.

HOOPER AGREES TO TAKE DOWN SIGNS
OPEN'G THE BEACHES

SC 30 EXT. PUBLIC · BEACH PARKING LOT (D)
NICE SUNNY DAY · LOT 1/2 FULL
6 OR SO CARS PULL IN — KIDS GET OUT
UNSTRAP SURFBOARDS — FAMILIES W/ TOWELS
COOLERS · BLANKETS · ETC. · HEAD TOWARD BEACH.

SC 31 EXT BEACH (D)
DOZENS OF PEOPLE ON BEACH · COOK'G HAM-
BURGER · TOSSING FRISBEES · ETC. FEW PEOPLE
SWIM'G — 4 KIDS ON RAFTS · WOMAN · IN BIKINI
TALK'G TO 6 YR OLD SON — ALEX PICK UP
RAFT — GOES IN WATER

SC 33 WOMAN WATCHES FOR A MOMENT THEN LAY BACK

SC 34 ALEX ON RAFT.
SC 35 P.O.V. FISH SEE'S RAFTS
SC 36 HELICOPTER SHOT OF SHAPE & RAFT.
SC 37 ALEX LOOKS TOWARD SHORE — PADDLE TO SHORE
SC 38 HEL. SHOT SHARK EXPLODES UNDER ALEX
TAKE'S HIM & RAFT INTO THE AIR.
SC 39 MAN ON BEACH LOOK'S OUT TO SEE — SEE
SOMETHING — NOT SURE
SC 40 ALEX'S MOTHER LOOK'S FOR HIM
SC 41 WAVE WASH — PIECES OF RAFT

SC 42 EXT. PUBLIC · BEACH PARKING LOT
3 CARS IN LOT — 2 FULL OF TEENAGER —
DRINK'G BEER ETC. — COP CAR — HENDRICKS
GETS OUT REMOVES SIGNS FR. TRUNK —
& STARTS TO HEAD FOR THE BEACH

43 EXT TOWN HALL PARKING LOT Ⓝ
BRODY'S CAR MOVES SLOWLY THRU. LOT LOOK'G
FOR SPACE - LOT JAMMED FULL CARS OF ALL
TYPES & SIZE.

44. INT. BRODY'S CAR Ⓝ
BRODY FINDS A SPACE - SITS FOR A MOMENT - TALK
TO ELLEN

45. INT. TOWN HALL Ⓝ
TOWN MEET'G IN NOISY PROGRESS - ABOUT 200
⁵⁰ PEOPLE IN THE HALL. ALL TYPES - IN THE FRONT
~~SEE~~ ARE 7 CHAIRS ON A RAISED PLATFORM.
VAUGHAN HEAD'G THE MEET'G. - HEATED MEET'G
DOOR OPENS AT THE REAR OF THE ROOM
ELLEN & BRODY ENTER. BRODY STANDS
UP AT THE FRONT OF THE ROOM - PEOPLE TALK
DECIDE TO LET BEN GARDNER TRY TO CATCH
THE FISH. HOOPER & BRODY TALK AS THE
PEOPLE FILE OUT OF THE HALL

51 EXT. DOCK Ⓝ
DOCK & HARBOR QUIET & DARK ONLY LIGHT
COMES FR. HARBORMASTERS SHACK - WE SEE HIM
SIT'G & READ'G INSIDE - ELTON COME DOWN
DOCK TOWARD SHACK - TURN TO A BLIP - THROWS
HIS - SACKS - ETC IN SMALL OUTBOARD BOAT.
MEN TALK A MOMENT - THEN - ELTON STARTS
ENGINE & SMALL BOAT MOVE OUT INTO THE DARKNESS

52 EXT. MIDDLE-CLASS RESIDENTIAL ST. (DAWN)
DAY BREAK'G - FOG DISSIPATING - SUN RAYS THRU
THE TREES - ST. EMPTY - DR. OPENS - MAN COMES
OUT W/ MARINE CORPS. GEAR - RIFLE - PISTOL ETC
GET INT CAR DR. & HOUSE DOWN PICKS UP MAN
WITH SPEAR GUN ETC.

53. INT PRATT'S CAR (DAWN)
SHOWS HAND GRENADES

54. EXT STREET (DAWN)
CAR DRIVES DO. ST. SEES OTHER CAR PARKED
BLINKS LIGHTS - IT FOLLOWS.

55. EXT. DRIVEWAY (DAWN)
2 MEN SIT'G IN PICKUP TRUCK - IN BACK OF
TRUCK FULL W/ BOW ARROWS - SHOTGUN CASE
2 FISHING RODS - AFRICAN SPEAR.

56 EXT. STREET (DAWN)
2 CAR TURN THE CORNER - BLINKS LIGHTS
PICKUP FALLS INTO LINE

57. EXT. HARBOR (DAWN)
DOCK IS QUIET ALL BOAT EMPTY - ENGINE
NOISE - CARAVAN OF CAR & TRUCKS TURN
CORNER - PULL UP TO DOCK. 20 MEN GET OUT
HUSTLE TOWARD DIFFERENT BOATS.

58 EXT. DOCK ⠀⠀⠀DAWN
AS WE HEAR THE BUSTLE & GROWL OF
MEN SHOUT'G - WE SEE ELTON COME AROUND
THE BEND INTO THE HARBOR

59 EXT. DOCK ⠀⠀⠀DAWN
HARBORMASTER COMES OUT - TALKS TO
ELTON

60 EXT. FISHING BOAT AT SEA ⒟
THE "FLICKA" - GARDNER & MATE - FISH'G FOR
SHARK. 2 RODS IN HOLDER - CALM SEA

61 FLYING BRIDGE - GARDNER SEES BOAT COMB'G

64. GARDNER FURIOUS OVER BOATS ARRIVE.
GLASSTRON ARRIVES 1ST HITS "FLICKA" W/ BOAT
2 OR 3 BOAT SURROUND "FLICKA"

65 FISH'G ROD BENT OVER - LINE CAUGHT ON ᴹᴼᵀᴼᴿ
GLASSTRON - CUT THRU SLICK - SPRAYS WATER ON FLICKA

68·70·72. GARDNER DECIDES TO GET OUT OF THE AREA.

74. NEW AREA NEAR FLOCK OF BIRDS - MATE HOOKS
A BLUE FISH

75. OTHER BOAT ARRIVE TO NEW SPOT START ATTACK
THE BLUEFISH - W/ SPEARS - GUNS - ETC.

78. MATE FIGHT'G W/ BLUEFISH - LAUGH'G AT
GLASSTRON SINK'G - SPEAR HITS BULKHEAD.

80 GARDNER DECIDES TO LEAVE - THROWS ROD OVER-
BOARD. GUNS ENGINES - TAKES OFF.

62 EXT. OCEAN ⒟
WE SEE FLOTILLA NEAR'G "FLICKA" - BOATS OF ALL TYPES

63 LEAD BOAT 16° GLASSTRON - PRAT & FELIX

67. BOATS SPEED OUT RAGTAG DISARRY -
NOBODY KNOWS HOW TO FISH. PLAY'G CHICKEN
W/ EACH OTHER.

69. 2 GUYS HOOK ON EACH OTHERS LINES.
- GUY BLAST LINES W/ SHOTGUN

71. WE SEE FLOCK OF TERNS DIVING A 100YD ᴼᵁᵀ
BLUEFISH BENEATH.

---

75. PRATT IN GLASSTRON - SEE'S MATE HOOK
BLUEFISH - PRATT TAKE OFF AFTER "FLICKA"

77. FELIX PICK UP GRENADE - BLOW UP GLASSTRON
BOAT BEGINS TO SINK.

79 ANOTHER BOAT PICKS UP FELIX

81 EXT. SHORE ⒟
QUINT W/ BINOCULAR - LAUGH'G AT FISHERMAN
PICK UP TRUCK NEXT HIM HAS A SHARK
PAINT ON THE DOOR.

82. OCEAN - PRATT. - FELIX. 2 OTHER MEN
STAND IN BOAT THAT PULLED OUT OF THE
WATER - WATCH'G THE "FLICKA" SPEED AWAY

83. 30 YDS AWAY 3 MEN IN A BOAT HOOK
LATE BLUEFISH. DORSAL FIN CAN BE SEEN

84. PRATT & FELIX GO TO BOAT W/ SHARK

85 MANY BOATS HAVE CIRCLED SHARK. HIT'G
IT W/ SPEARS - SHOOT'G IT ETC.

86 PRATT MOVE UP TO THE SHARK - FIRES
3 SHOTS INTO IT. FISH STOPS TRASH'G
THEY PULL THE SHARK ABOARD - SLIT ITS
BELLY OPEN - FELIX SAID HE SAW A BOUE.
THEY HEAD FOR SHORE.

87 EXT. STREET
HOOPER'S PICKUP SPEED'G ALONG THE STREET
MAKE A LEFT TURN - RACING TOWARDS THE
DOCK - AT THE DOCK LARGE CROWD
SEVERAL CARS - BRODYS POLICE CAR -
HOOPER PULLS UP - GOES TO CROWD.

88 EXT. DOCK ⒟
SHARK HUNG ON A OVERHEAD POLE -
MAN GATHERED AROUND HAVING PICTURE
TAKEN - HOOPER TALK W/ VAUGHAN -
THEY THINK THEY'VE GOT THE GREAT WHITE.
HOOPER PULLS DO. HIS PANTS - SHOWS
BRODY ~~SCAR~~ SCAR OF BLUE SHARK BITE.
- TELLS HIM THAT IS NOT THE RIGHT SHARK
BRODY LOOKS AT SLIPS - SEE A SLIP
SIGN OVER IT "BEN GARDNERS "FLICKA" FOR
DAY CHARTERS.

89 EXT. PUBLIC - BEACH PARKING LOT (EE)
HENDRICKS COM'G FR. DUNES W/ SIGNS
- THROWS THEM IN TRUNK OF POLICE CAR.

90. ᴱˣᵀ OCEAN & HOOPERS RENTED BOAT ⒟
HOOPER IN RENTED BOAT HEAD'G AWAY
FR. HARBOR - HOOPER - TALK ON RADIO
- LOOK FOR THE "FLICKA" - SEE A BOAT IN THE ~~DISTAL~~

91. HELICOPTER SHOT - HOOPER APPROACH'G QUINT'S
BOAT.

92. HOOPER · P.O.V. QUINT MACHINE GUN'G
SEAGULLS.

93 EXT FLICKA - ~~AND HOOPERS~~ BOAT
~~HALF FULL~~ OF WATER
HOOPER APPROACHES FLICKA - SEE ~~NOBODY~~
NOBODY ABOARD - GET INTO HIS SCUBA
GEAR GOES UNDERWATER.

95. HOOPER PULLS HIMSELF ABOARD -
SHARKS TOOTH IN HIS HAND 3" LONG
GOES ABOARD "FLICKA" - HE FIND BEN
BODY FLOAT'G IN HIS CABIN - PULLS IT OUT
- GOES TO HIS BOAT & RADIOS.

94 EXT. UNDERWATER ⒟
HOOPER DESCENDS - WE SEE UNDERSIDE
OF BOAT - HOLE SIZE OF A BASKETBALL -
TAKE KNIFE - DIGS OUT SHARKS TOOTH.

96 EXT. DOCK ⒟
BRODY - HOOPER STAND'G ON DOCK
2 - AMBULANCE PERSONNEL HAUL GARDNER'S
BODY OUT OF BOAT ON STRETCHER -
TOWARDS AMBULANCE. HOOPER SHOWS BRODY
SHARKS TOOTH - THEY WALK TO HOOPERS
TRUCK. HOOPER SKETCH A WHITE SHARK
BRODY - ~~CUT THE SHARK DOWN~~ HANG

97 EXT PUBLIC BEACH PARKING LOT ⒟
LATE AFTERNOON - KIDS LASH'G SURFBOARDS
TO CARS - ETC. - HENDRICKS PULL IN - TAKES
OUT SIGNS AGAIN - WALK TOWARDS BEACH.

98 EXT ROUTE 27 ⒟
GAS STATION - ROAD SIGN - "AMITY" -
RIGHT TURN - EAST HAMPTON - STRAIGHT AHEAD.
PEOPLE TELL STATION MAN - NOT GOING TO AMITY

101 EXT. DOWNTOWN AMITY ⒟
LANE OF ELEGANT SHOPS - BOUTIQUES -
ST. IS EMPTY - WOMAN CARRY'G "END OF SEASON SALE"
SIGN - "EVERYTHING HALF PRICE"

102. POLICEMAN WALK'G - CHARTERED BUS PULLS UP.
PEOPLE W/ CAMERAS ETC. DRIVE ASKS WHERE
SHARK BEACH IS -

FORM NUMBER GEN. 5

103 EXT. MOVIE THEATER (D)
"MOBY DICK" RUNNING - PEOPLE IN BOTH'G SUITS
- SHORTS ETC. STAND'G IN LINE.

104 INT. MOVIE THEATER (D)
CROWDED - EXCEPT FOR AROUND QUINT.
HE'S LAUGH'G. EAT'G POPCORN - SHOT OF
AHAB - JABB'G THE WHALE.

105 INT. POLICE STATION (D)
~~BOB~~ BRODY SITT'G IN OFFICE w/ HOOPER
ON PHONE - FINDS OUT GARDNER DIED OF
HEART ATTACK.

106 EXT. PUBLIC BEACH PARK'G LOT. (D)
LOT JAMMED w/ CARS - BRODY'S CAR
PARKED BY PATH TO BEACH - A BLACK
SEDAN PULLS UP. BEHIND BRODYS CAR -
"WNBC NEWS" - PAINTED ON DOOR - MAN
GETS OUT TALKS TO BRODY - OTHER NEWS
MEN GET OUT — PEOPLE TALK TO
BRODY ABOUT BUY SELL'G TICKETS.

107 EXT. BEACH (D)
WE SEE T.V. CREW SETT'G UP - BRODY
WALK'G ALONG BEACH TALKS TO HOOPER
ON WALKIE-TALKIE - HOOPER ON BOAT.

108 EXT. HOOPER'S BOAT (D)
HOOPER STAND'G ON STERN OF BOAT.

109 INT. PATROL CAR (D)
HENDRICKS ON PHONE

110 EXT SIDE STREET.
GUY SELL'G TICKETS AT TABLE - SEE
HENDRICKS - JUMPS UP - HENDRICKS PUTS
HIM IN BACK SEAT OF POLICE CAR.

---

111 EXT BEACH D
TEENAGERS TALK'G ABOUT BET TO GO
INTO WATER.

SEE 112 TO 123 - BOY IN WATER
SHAPE OF FISH COMES AFTER HIM.

124 INT. BRODY OFFICE (N)
BRODY - HOOPER - VAUGHAN - MEADOW
TALK ABOUT GETT'G QUINT.

125 EXT. BRODY'S CAR. (N)
CAR TOOL'G ALONG 27. HEAVY TRAFFIC
- SIGNALS TO TO LEFT AT SIGN
"PROMISED LAND".

126 INT. BRODYS CAR (N)
INSIDE CAR LOOK'G OUT - BAD ROAD
- COME TO - SMALL DARK TOWN - GAS STATION
GENERAL STORE - BOY CLOSED.
BRODY - HOOPER TALK. - BRODY
TURNS DOWN A REAL BAD ROAD -
RUTS - SOIL - COVER w/ FOLIAGE. WE COME
TO A CLEAR'G - RAMSHACKLE HOUSE - ON THE
RIGHT - THE FLY'G BRIDGE OF 45' BOAT.

127 EXT. QUINTS PROPERTY (N)
127 DOCK - SHACK OF A HOUSE - BOAT.
THEY GO TO DOCK. - GO ABOARD BOAT.

129 INT QUINTS BOAT.
130 INT OF BOAT FILLED w/ JUNK - HOOKS - HARPOONS
SHARK JAWS - ETC. - QUINT - BRODY - HOOPER TALK
HAVE DRINK OF RYE

---

131 EXT QUINTS DOCK.
HOOPER DRUNK - SEES NAME OF BOAT
"ORCA"
132 THEY WALK UP TO THE CAR.
133 - 137. LOBSTER FISHER MAN SEQ.

138 - 153 ABOARD THE ORCA.
SEE OTHER BREAK' DOWN

172. INT. BRODY KITCHEN (N)
ELLEN MAKING DRINKS

173. INT. BRODY LIVING ROOM (N)
BRODY SITTING ON COUCH - THEY HAVE
BEEN HAVING A ARGUMENT - ELLEN CRY'G
TURNS AND RUNS UPSTAIRS.

FORM NUMBER GEN. 5 (BOY ON RAFT SEQ.)
(LARGE UNDER WATER
SHAPE OF FISH ~~BREAKING~~ WATER NEEDED
DAY BREAKING
SC. 31 32 DOZENS OF PEOPLE ON THE BEACH
FAMILIES COOKING HAMBURGERS - TEENAGERS
LYING ON THE BEACH - COLLEGE KIDS
TOSSING FRISBEES - PEOPLE SWIMMING
IN THE SURF. - A KIDS ON A RAFTS
FLOAT JUST BEYOND SURF LINE. A WOMAN
IN A BIKINI LYING ON HER BACK -
6 YR OLD SON - ASK HER TO LET HIM
GO INTO THE WATER - SHE FINALLY AGREES
TO LET HIM GO IN. - HE PICK UP 4/5' RAFT
WADES INTO SURF BEGINS PADDLE & KRK.
33 EXT. BEACH
HIS MOTHER - WATCHES FOR A WHILE THEN
TURN BACK TO HER TOWEL.
34 EXT. WATER.
ALEX IS ALONE - 30 YDS FR. NEAREST
OTHER PERSON ON A RAFT - PADDLING AWAY
FROM SHORE - CAMERA STAYS ON HIM
FOR A MOMENT THEN TRAVELS BEYOND HIM,
SEAWARD. WATER IS CALM. NOW WE
SEE SAME OMINOUS RIPPLE THAT WE SAW
w/ CHRIS.
35 EXT. UNDERWATER. - D
SHARK P.O.V. WE SEE PEOPLE LYING
ON RAFTS - OUTLINE RAFTS - w/ ARMS & LEGS
DANGLING IN THE WATER. WE TRAVEL FROM
RAFT TO RAFT. THEN THERE IS A SPACE
OF OPEN WATER - THEN QUICK SHOT OF
A SINGLE RAFT. (ALEX'S RAFT)

36 EXT. HELICOPTER TYPE SHOT
LOOKING DOWN ON THE WATER WE
SEE THE RAFT FLOAT'G - WE RECOGNIZE

ALEX'S RAFT BY IT'S COLOR. - WE SEE A
LARGE GREY SHAPE THAT DWARFS THE
RAFT. IT CIRCLES THE RAFT, AND DIVE DOWN.
37. ALEX IS LYING QUIETLY ON THE RAFT
LOOKS TOWARDS SHORE - NOTICES THAT'S
HE'S GOTTEN PRETTY FAR OUT - STARTS PADDLING
& KICKING TOWARD THE BEACH.

38. EXT. WATER.
ALEX IS PADDLING TOWARDS US - SUDDENLY
THE SHARK EXPLODES FROM THE WATER
SEIZING ALEX & THE RAFT IN HIS JAWS.
ABOUT HALF OF THE SHARK CLEARS THE WATER
ALEX & THE RAFT SMASHED BETWEEN THE
TEETH. WE HEAR THE SOUND OF AIR
RUSH'G FR. THE RAFT. FOAM & BLOOD & WATER
SPEWS FR. THE SHARKS MOUTH.

39. EXT. BEACH D.
A MAN HAS BEEN PLAYING w/ HIS DAUGHTER
IN THE SURF - HE HEARD SOMETHING, HE
LOOK OUT TO SEA - WE SEE WHAT HE
SEES - A FLASH OF SOMETHING MONSTROUS -
FOLLOWED BY A TREMENDOUS SPLASH.
40. - ALEX - MOTHER OPENS HER EYES HEARS
THE COMMOTION. SHE THE MAN POINTING
OUT. TO SEA, STARTS CALLING ALEX.
41 EXT. WAVE WASH D.
PIECES OF RUBBER RAFT FLOAT TO SHORE
IT'S CAUGHT IN A SMALL WAVE AND
WASHES TO SHORE
42.

FORM NUMBER GEN. 5 (BOY GOES OUT ON BET
112-113 LARGE FIN & MOVING TAIL NEEDED)
EXT. BEACH. D. & WATER.
BRODY SITT'G ON DUNE, LOOKING OUT TO SEA.
SUDDENLY CHEER FR. CROWD - JIMMY
SPRINTS FOR THE WATER - STARTS TO SWIM -
BRODY YELLS AT HIM. - HOOPER IN BOAT
TALKS TO BRODY - PUTS WALKIE-TALKIE AD.
STARES AT WATER FOR A MOMENT - LOOK
PERPLEXED. THEN RAM THROTTLE FORWARD
PUT THE BOAT IN A TIGHT TURN TOWARDS
SHORE - WE LINGER ON THE WATER - THEN
WE SEE THE HUMP RISE IN THE WATER.
114 EXT. BEACH.
115 LARGE CROWD GATHERING - T.V. STATION
PHOTOGRAPHING - BRODY TELLING THE KID
TO COME IN.
116 BRODY STANDS KNEE DEEP IN THE SURF.
BOY SWIM'G FOR SHORE HOOPER'S BOAT
CATCHING UP.
117 HOOPERS BOAT.
HOOPER. STAND'G IN COCKPIT. WATCH'S BOY
SWIM FOR SHORE. SOMETHING CATCHES HIS EYE.
INSERT. SILVER GREY STREAK. HUGE.
118 SHOT. HOOPER FACE LOOK'G SHOCKED.
118 EXT. BEACH.
BRODY HEARS HOOPER CALL - BRODY RUN INTO
WATER 10-15 YDS FROM JIMMY -
119. JIMMY HEARS HOOPER - HE PANIC START
TO THRASH
120. BEACH & NEWS MEN
121 SURF BRODY STRUGGLING CLOSER. -
WE SEE GRAY FIN RISE
122 BEACH PEOPLE SEE FIN - THRASHING TAIL
123 BRODY - GRABS BOY - FOR A SECOND FIN PURSUES
THEM - WARY OF SHALLOW WATER - VEERS OFF/BOY IN.

Panel 1 (top left)

LOBSTER FISHERMAN
(WHOLE SHARK ON LONG ARM - LIFTED)

133) EXT. AMITY HARBOR (N)
ELTON, LOBSTER FISHERMAN IS PREPARING
TO GO OUT TO CHECK HIS TRAPS - STANDING
AT SKIFF, CHECKING EQUIPMENT / HARBOR-
MASTER COME OUT OF HIS SHACK AS ELTON
UNTIES HIS LINES. / - TALK TO ELTON - /
- ELTON STARTS MOTOR UNTIES LAST
LINE - PUSHES OFF FRO DOCK / MOVE
SLOWLY OUT TO SEA - WE LOSE HIM IN
THE NIGHT. /
134) EXT SEA. LOW MIST HANGING OVER
WATER - ELTON'S SKIFF COMES SLOWLY
INTO VIEW - / IT PASSES THRU A CUT WHERE
THE WATER IS SLIGHTLY ROUGHER, THEN
MOVES INTO CALM OPEN WATER - / HE LOCATES
HIS FIRST TRAP. PULLS IT UP / TAKE OUT
TO LOBSTER. - REBAITS - DROPS TRAP OVER
BOARD. / HE MOVE OFF. / APPROACHES ANOTHER
POT BUOY / SHIFTS HIS MOTOR INTO NEUTRAL /
HAUL ON THE TRAP / BUT IT SEEM TO BE
CAUGHT ON SOMETHING - TO GET MORE
LEVERAGE, HE KNEELS ON THE SLAT SEAT
AND LEANS FAR OVERBOARD / WE HEAR A
HISS IN THE WATER - FOLLOWED BY A SLAP
- SLAP SPLASHING SOUND / ELTON HEAR THE
NOISE & TURNS / INSERT ELTON'S FACE /
HORRIFIED /
135) CAMERA IS BEHIND SKIFF LOOK'G
FORWARD - ELTON IS SIT'G W/ HIS BACK TO
US. RIGID IN TERROR / COMING TOWARD THE BOW
GREAT SHARK - JAWS -OPEN - HITS BOW OF SKIFF /
DRAWS IT UNDERWATER - W/ A SMOOTH

Panel 2 (top middle)

FLUID MOTION GRAB ELTON / TAKEN
2/3 OF HIS BODY IN HIS MOUTH / - CONTIN-
UING. THE SHARK PASSES OVER THE BOAT
TAKING ELTON WITH HIM. /
136) EMPTY SKIFF - AWASH MOVE SLOWLY
IN A TIGHT CIRCLE ON THE WATER - THE
ENGINE CONTINUES TO PURR QUIETLY /
137)

Panel 3 (top right)

1st TIME at SEA w/ Quint - Brody - Hooper
154 - 171
need top of fish's mouth
154 EXT. SEA (D) open
Long shot of 'ORCA
sitting as a paper cup in a puddle - It is past
noon but the heat is still intense. there is no
motion in the sea, or on the boat. A tern dives
into the chum slick and rises again.

155 EXT. ON FLYING BRIDGE (D)
Quint sits on the bench, staring at the slick
He takes a long pull at a beer, empties the can
pegs it overboard. It hits the water and drifts
slowly aft. Quint watches the can for a few
seconds, but then something catches his eye
and he snaps his head back toward the slick.

156 EXT. BOAT D.
Brody has been dozing in the fighting chair, He
jerks awake and sees the line next to him
beginning to feed out. slowly at first,
then more rapidly

157. EXT. BOAT D.
Quint swings down from the flying bridge,
takes rod from holder puts it in between
Brody's legs. - note various shots of line
in the water - snarls. loops etc. + Quint
examines line.

158. EXT. BOAT
The reaction is as if Quint had set off a
firecracker - Hooper jumps off the transom
excited -

Panel 4 (bottom left)

the 3 men stand silently watching the water,
then the pot line begins to run. Brody move to
take the rod but Quint puts a hand on this
shoulder and stops him.

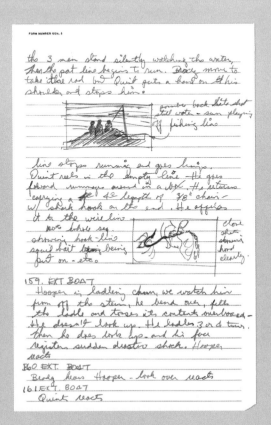

somber back lit shot
still water - sun playing
off fishing line

line stops running and goes limp.
Quint reels in the empty line. He goes
forward rummages around in a box. He returns
carrying a 4° length of 3/8" chain -
w/ shark hook on the end. He applies
it to the wire line
note whole seq.
showing hook - line
squid bait being being
put on - etc.
close
shot
showing
hook
clearly.

159. EXT BOAT
Hooper is ladling chum. we watch him
from off the stern, he bends over, fills
the ladle and tosses its contents overboard -
the dresn't look up. He ladles a 2nd time.
then he does look up. and his face
registers sudden drastic shock. Hooper
reacts
160 EXT. BOAT
Brody hears Hooper - look over reacts
161 EXT. BOAT
Quint reacts

Panel 5 (bottom middle)

165 BOAT
Brody holding rifle. Hooper stares off stern
Quint comes aft carrying 2 barrels, with
coils of ropes and harpoon barbs attached.
As he sets barrels on transom - tells to
men - take another step on the ladder -
suddenly we hear swishing noise, a liquid
hiss - Quint points to water
166 EXT. SEA (D)
30° off port side we see dorsal fin
at least 2° high knifing the water
toward the boat. It is followed by a
towering tail that swirls left and right in
a tight cadence

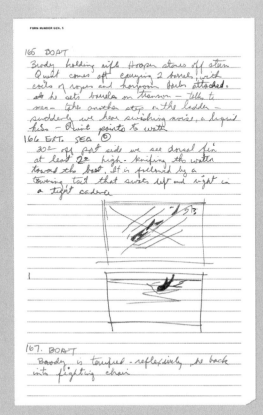

167. BOAT
Brody is terrified - reflexively, he back
into fighting chair

Panel 6 (bottom right)

Quint hops down from ladder and dashes
for stern - fumbles w/ harpoon

168 EXT. SEA (D)
fish almost at boat - lifts its
head out of water - we see big black eye
gazing upward - head dips and fish
passes under boat
169 BOAT
Quint hasn't seen the fish pass under
the boat, he raises the harpoon for a
throw, but he's pointing it at the side from
which the fish has already moved -
Quint turns, but as he does so, the harpoon
shaft strikes the back of the fighting chair
dislodging the barb which clatters to the deck
170. SEA
we see the shark move away from the
starboard side. tail slashing in the water
171 BOAT
Quint drops harpoon - grabs rifle
squeezes off all 8 shots in clip - in a
futile rage. fish has gone. - puts down
rifle and laughs
Quint takes a note pad and pencil from
a shirt pocket points his left arm
toward shore then scribbles something on pad
- taking bearings - shot of what Quint
is taking bearings of - we barely see anything

2nd TIME OUT - QUINT-HOOPER-BRODY

174. EXT. QUINT'S DOCK. (D)
IT is early morning. boat is ready to go.
Brody - Hooper, Quint are standing on dock
between them sits a aluminum cage - in the
cage are scuba tanks etc. - The men talk.
Quint agrees to let Hooper bring the cage
aboard - the 3 men hail the cage and
on board.

75. EXT. BOAT
the ORCA sits almost still in the calm
water. Quint is on the flying bridge. Brody
sits on the transom ladling chum.
Hooper is fiddling w/ something in the
cage which has been tucked in a corner.
sun is high. Brody go down the ladder
into cabin to get beer.

175A. INTO CABIN (D)
Brody come down ladder - goes to ice chest
take out beer. we hear Quint voice "there it is"

176. EXT. BOAT
Brody come out of cabin stand look. "where"
- "Deal off stern"

177. EXT SEA
from stern of boat we look aft. - 30-
40 - yds - see Dorsal Fin and Caudal Fin.
the fish seems to be meandering slowly
going nowhere.

---

maybe 2 shots

178. EXT. BOAT
Quint comes down from flying bridge
starts forward - "tells Brody to bring line in
Brody reels in line Hooper stands still -
stands at fish which we can see in the
distance - Quint returns from the bow,
carrying a barrel - coil of rope - harpoon -
sets the barrel on the transom & climbs up-
stands on transom legs spread - harpoon
resting on his shoulder. - Quint yells at
fish - 3 men wait - (we maybe cut back
to over shark shot at last - slightly different)
shark just stays out there does not come
closer.
They talk about use porpoise bait - Quint
hope down goes over to garbage can take off
lid hand, porpoise out - takes it off.
from the lazaret he take a length of dog
leash chain. to the other end of chain he
ties a heavy rope which he fasten to a cleat.
He again mounts transom - carrying
porpoise up him. - hold porpoise over
board slashes its belly - a rank -
dark liquid oozes out fall on water

D
162 EXT. SEA
from stern we see shark not 10° off of stern
- conical snout sticking out of water and
2° mouth is not quite half way open
a dim cavern guarded by huge triangular
teeth

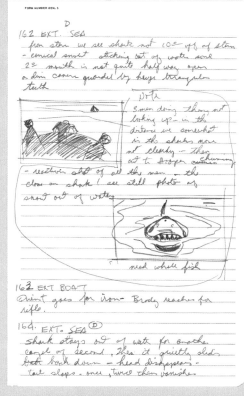

Note
3 men doing thing not
looking up - in the
distance we somewhat
see the sharks more
or less not clearly - then
cut to Hooper scuba
- reaction shot of all the men - then
close on shark! see still photo of
snout out of water

need whole fish

162 EXT BOAT
Quint goes for iron - Brody reaches for
rifle.

164. EXT. SEA (D)
shark stays out of water for another
couple of second, then it quietly slides
back back down - head disappears -
tail slaps - once, twice then vanishes.

Quint tosses porpoise overboard - lets out
of feet of rope - and stands on
the rest - preventing it from feeding out
- He hoist his harpoon (note detail shots
of rope - porpoise - etc.

179. EXT. SEA
The shark moves in quickly - 20-15-10
yds away - fin stops moving - tail vanishes
dorsal fin drops backward. great head
rears up - mouth open in a slack savage
grin - eyes black & abysmal

180 EXT. BOAT
Brody face shown horror - Hooper is awed -
Quint stands on transom harpoon raised
legs spread - fish is off stern, slightly
to port - porpoise has been hung off
starboard -

181 - THE SEA.
head & flanks stays out for another
second the soundlessly slip back and
disappears

182. EXT. BOAT
Brody - Quint pointing harpoon at porpoise
- boat suddenly lurches violently to one
side - shark has struck on the port
side - Quint legs skid out from under
him and he falls on his back on the
transom - Brody tumbles sideways - hits
fighting chair Hooper slams into port gunwal

---

188. EXT. BOAT
Quint & Brody looking overboard at
the cage.

189. EXT. UNDERWATER.
we are in the cage w Hooper.
bubbly froth of his descent has
disappeared. A thong holds the powerhead
to his right arm. Another thong holds
a camera to his left arm. We hear the
sound of his breathing. water is clear.
shafts of sunlight stretch downward
in the blue. there is nothing around.
a number of angles needed. close, long etc.
check "cousteau" for color photo - for mood.
may be large color illustration needed here also.

Suddenly from the deep gloom - rising
slowly - smoothly - comes the shark.
It moves with no apparent effort.
sinuous beyond belief. powerful and sleek
as a submarine.
We watch it from Hooper's P.O.V.
the shark moves in, cruising effortlessly,
as it near the cage. it turns, and its
great length passes right in front of her
noses. first the snout, then the jaws
slack and smiling, then the black eye.
Hooper reaches out with his hand and
touches the vinyl flesh, letting his
fingertips caress the shark until at the
last moment. the huge tail slaps then away

---

we should do many angles. possible other
the fish at Hooper - cut in close on Hooper face)
a continuous shot nose to tail moving slowly
across the PAN-A-VIEW screen. - insert Hoopers
hand as large grey field goes by

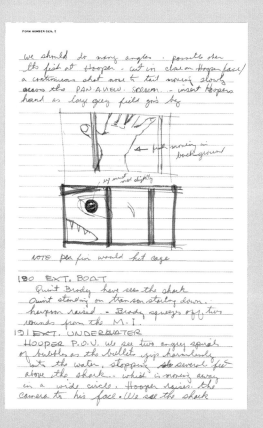

NOTE sea fin would hit cage

190. EXT. BOAT
Quint Brody have see the shark
Quint standing on transom staring down.
harpoon raised - Brody squeezes off two
rounds from the M-I

191 EXT. UNDERWATER
HOOPER P.O.V. we see two angry spirals
of bubbles as the bullets zip harmlessly
into the water, stopping several feet
above the shark, which is moving away
in a wide circle. Hooper raises the
camera to his face. We see the shark

continue its wide arc, turning back now
toward the cage. It move slowly at first,
the suddenly speeds up, the great tail
thrashing wildly, driving the body
forward. Hooper in position, expecting
the shark to turn.

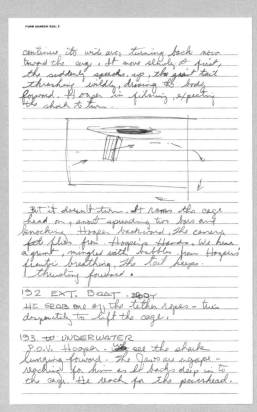

But it doesn't turn. It rams the cage
head on, snout spreading two bars and
knocking Hooper backward. The camera
falls flies from Hooper's hands. We hear
a grunt, mingled with bubbles from Hooper's
frantic breathing, the tail keeps
thrusting forward.

192 EXT. BOAT. BODY
HE GRAB one of the tether ropes - tries
desperately to lift the cage.

193 UNDERWATER
P.O.V. Hooper. we see the shark
lunging forward - the Jaws are agape -
reaching for him as he backs deep into
the cage. He reach for the powerhead.

194 UNDERWATER
from outside the cage we see Hooper
tries to ward it off. but at his attempts
is as futile as trying to stop a freight
train with a fly swatter. the shark turns
on its side grab Hooper tries in its
mouth, the mouth bite down, nearly
cutting Hooper in two. its start to drag
him out of the cage.

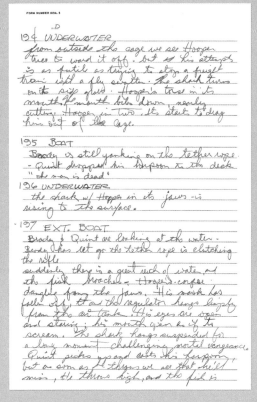

195 BOAT
Brody is still yanking on the tether rope.
- Quint drops his harpoon to the deck
"the man is dead"

196 UNDERWATER
the shark w/ Hooper in its jaws - is
rising to the surface.

197 EXT. BOAT
Brody & Quint are looking at the water.
Brody has let go the tether rope is clutching
the rifle
suddenly there is a great rush of water, and
the fish breaches - Hooper's corpse
dangle from the jaws. His mask has
fallen off, and the regulator hangs limply
from the air tank. His eyes are open
and staring; his mouth open as if to
scream. The shark hangs suspended for
a long moment challenging mortal vengeance.
Quint picks up and casts the harpoon,
but as soon as it thrown we see that he'll
miss, the throws high, and the fish is

already beginning to slide beneath the
water - Brody fire two quick shots, the first
hits the water in front of the fish. The
second hits Hooper in the neck.
Quint jumps down and grabs the rifle from
Brody, he whips it up to his shoulder
and fire two more shots, to late, the shark
has slid back under water. the bullets slap
in its wake. the two men stand there
riveted, the water colors down quickly.
There is no sign of the fish any there.
In a fury, Quint he pulls the knife from his
sheath and slashes the rope holding the
cage. w/ a brief sucking sound, the cage dips
away - Brody is near tears, trembling in shock
fear & grief. Quint jumps upon transom - shouting
his going to kill the fish.

198 EXT. BOAT
Brody thinks Quint has gone crazy - picks
up rifle. points it at Quint tells him there
going in - Quint laughs a him jumps around
- tell Brody to start chumming - Brody does so

199 EXT. SEA - Twilight
It is almost dark. we are 50 yards from
the boat, as it drifts silently. The light
is on the cabin. We see the dim figure
of Brody - ladeling chum - Quint
fiddling with a fishing line.

200
Brody watches Quint as he baits a fishing line.
Quint finish baits the hook. Throw it
overboard, let out some line.

201 EXT. BOAT (N)
Quint hauls in bonito - begin cutting up
the fish. He lays the fillets on the gun
wale, put up the carcass - sucks out the
fish's eyes. - offers the other one to Brody
- Brody take out notch lifts
lifts it and holds it under the fish fillet
- good dramatic light effect here

202. EXT. THE SEA (N)
we see the boat in the distance a couple
of hundred yards away. camera travels
across the still water, as it travels we see
the ripples of the great fish moving
beneath the surface.

203. EXT. BOAT (N)
Brody asleep - in fighting chair - awakened
by - jarring of boat. - Quint jumps down
for the flying bridge grab harpoon.

204 EXT. BOAT Dawn
Brody in fighting chair - cold comes creeps
around him dawn is breaking - Quint
tells him to start chumming -. Brody
chum'g hear strange sound, look up -
see the shark.

205 Brody P.O.V. of shark a few feet
away.

206 Quint leap f. bridge grab harpoon.

207 EXT. SEA
Sharks head slips back in to water

208 Quint standing on transom - boat
hit head. Quint stumbles

209 EXT OVER STERN Down
fish, jaws clamped down on stern - shaking

210 Boat
Quint falls to his knees - the boat
lies still in the water. Brody good
down the hatch cover - /out of water?
close cover.

211 BOAT (D)
Quint on transom. we see dorsal fin
off starboard stern. moving fast toward the
boat - 6 or 8 ft away Quint throws
a harpoon.

212 OFF STERN
harpoon hit fish front of dorsal fin -
above away hits boat!

213 Quint! fall back - cut head on chair.

214. SEA.
we see barrel hit water dress'd stop
plunges beneath surface and vanishes.

215. Boat
Brody & Quint wait for barrels to rise
- we see barrel rise ten yards from boat.

216 EXT. STERN
fish breaks water in barrel - rises like a
rocket - white belly - (cheaper) Quint
sto hits in the belly with harpoon; he
gun down, (DO NOT shot CAUSE FAR)

217. EXT. BOAT
Quint & Brody in cockpit - watching
barrel go over, Quint start engine.
- Quint look are aft

218 EXT. OFF STERN
Barrels start chasing boat.

219. BOAT
Close on Quint - concern - anger - stops engine

220. EXT. SEA
boat about 20ge away. Quint rose out of
cockpit. go run forward - Brody walk to stern
barrels approach boat. from stern. On the
bow Quint frantically assembles harpoon.

218 BOAT.
Barrels draw near Brody braces himself.
anticipating thumps -

222 OVER STERN.
Brody P.O.V. see grey shape pass under
boat

223. Brody turn toward bow

224. Bow
Quint w/ harpoon. see grey shape
as it pulls away -

225. PULPIT.
Quint has harpoon raised - we see grey
shape - pull out of range. / Quint looks
down see barrels scrap along bow of ship/
- barrel stop - fish turns - head raises
out of water - 25 yds away -
- insert (shark head out of water. seems
as always to grin). head dips back -
tail starts thrashing. shark charges.
when shark is almost upon boat Quint
casts iron - we see fish no iron strikes
just over left eye. the mouth snaches

cuts the bow - teeth clamp down on the wsole

227. EXT. PULPIT.
Barrel pop overboard.

228 FLYING BRIDGE
Brody - stands at Andy - Quint in Pulpit. - barrels sink o - boat trembles - seeming to rise up - drop back - barrels pop up again two on one side one on the other - submerge again - the appear 20 yds away.
Brody starts down the ladder -

229. BOW
Quint hands Brody harpoon - goes down below. Brody walk out to the pulpit - look at barrel - Quint reappears wiping his hands on his pants.

230. SEA.
boat about 50 yds away tracking barrels. we can barely see them.

231. SEA
tight on barrels - motionless - boat approaches we pan up see Brody leaning on gunwale looking down at barrels.

232. BOAT.
Boat has stop. Quint Brody on starboard gunwale looks at barrel. Quint started playing w/ wrench, grab rope haul in barrel - bow - cut of barrel. feet rope thru pulley on gin pole tie to winch. - start pulling in fish - boat leaning hard to starboard. suddenly pick up straight - rope around foot. snarl around winch - Quint dashes for control panel throws throttle forward.

---

233. Boat
Quint two lots - fish breaks water right beside boat - rising with great whooshing noise - rises vertically - fall on stern - w/ a crash - narrowly missing Brody - It drive the stern underwater - water pours over transom - Quint & Brody standing hip deep. Shark lies there. Brody can see himself in fishes eye. Quint charge the fist w/ a fury, barrels & rope gathered around him - plunge harpoon in the belly many times. Blood pours from wounds. Boat begin to sink - stern falls - shark begin to roll off - dragging rope - suddenly Quint fell backwards - in water ("get knife"), his left leg comes out of water we see he is caught in the ropes

234.
EXT. SINKING BOAT
Brody struggle thru deep water to get knife - he grabs knife. turn back toward Quint no chance of reaching Quint in time. Every step Brody takes, Quint is dragged deep -. Quint disappear w/ shark!

234A. SEA.
P.O.V. of shark coming toward him - shark comes closer. Brody start hitting the shark on the nose. then close his so eye - screen goes black - regain see shark sinking underwater.

235A UNDER WATER.
P.O.V. SHARK & Quint tied to him

---

underwater, Quint eyes & mouth open. Brody raise & his head out.

236. SEA.
Brody alone in water - save for 3 bobbing barrels - grabs seat cushion - begins to kick toward shore.

237. SEA.
camera pulls away showing lone figures kicking in open sea.

THINGS TO CHECK FOR.
BOATS - QUINTS. HOOPERS RENTED ONE GAROUDERS - LOBSTER FISHERMAN - (MATCH BOTTOM)
QUINTS

·MAPS·
COVES - OCEAN DEPTH· TIDES· WEATHER
LIGHTHOUSES   SURF

MOTEL ETC. FOR CREW

HOUSES ON BEACH (SC 1)

SPECIAL THINGS ON BEACH/

SEAWEED

EXT. SO. SHORE. LONG ISLAND.? SC. 1-4 7-10   D/H
EXPENSIVE HOUSES. DUNES. BEACH.

EXT. PUBLIC· BEACH PARKING LOT. S-11,30 D
LOT BEHIND DUNES. PATH TO BEACH   S.H. 42,89,97,106

EXT. PRIVATE BEACH   SC.10.   P

EXT. MAIN STREET.   SC.17, 101,102
BOUTIQUE - POLICE STATION - MOVIE THEATER
SIDE ST. - HOTEL   SToN

EXT. ORIENT POINT - FERRY DOCK   D
                    SC. 18,

EXT. ABELARD ARMS HOTEL   D
OLD VICTORIAN BUILDING S.H. SC. 20

EXT. AMITY HARBOR   SC.25,28,51,57   D/N
HARBORMASTERS SHACK, DOCK. 58,59,81,96,88,133

EXT. PUBLIC BEACH   SC. 34-41,107-111-128 D

EXT. MIDDLE·CLASS RESIDENTIAL STREET.
DRIVEWAY. S.H.   SC. 52-56   (DANA)

EXT. TOWN HALL PARKING LOT.   (N)
BRODY - ELLEN IN CAR. S.H.   SC. 43-44

EXT. SHORE   SC 81   D
QUINT WATCHING w/ BINOCULARS

EXT. STREET   SC. 87   D
HOOPER RACING TO DOCK

EXT. MOVIE THEATER   NN SC.103   D

EXT. BRODY'S CAR - HWY 27 TURNS OFF   N
                    SC. 124,125,126

EXT. ROUGH ROAD
LEADING TO QUINTS PROPERTY   N
                    SC 126

EXT. QUINT - HOUSE - DOCK - BOAT   N
OLD SHACK, DOCK, ETC.   SC. 127-128, 131-132

INT BRODY'S HOUSE
          BEDROOM - SC 5   DAWN
          KITCHEN - SC 172   N
          LIVING RM. SC 173   N

INT. POLICE STATION
          BRODY'S OFFICE SC 12,29,105,124 D/N

INT. ABELARD ARMS   D
          LOBBY -   SC 21.

INT. ROOM 206   SC 23   D
          BATHROOM   SC 24

INT. HARBORMASTERS SHACK SC 26 DAWN
          ON AMITY HARBOR

INT. TOWN HALL   S.45-50   N

INT MOVIE THEATER SC 104   D

INT. QUINTS BOAT SC. 129,130   N

DISCOVERING AMITY ISLAND

AGAIN, THE CORE RESPONSIBILITY of a production designer is to envision a style, a tone, and a mood for a production. No matter how large or how small, regardless of how elaborate or how simple, the production designer's duty is to interpret, envision, and then enable a production to commence. And since Joe Alves had successfully assembled a team to wrangle construction of the great white shark, it now was time to tackle his next duty as designer: to create the setting.

As JAWS was initially considered to be a movie of only moderate import, Alves was, so far, running a one-man art department (aside from the industrious Magnificent Seven, now hard at work in Sunland, California). So when it came time to find a location to stage this show, Alves would set off on his own to locate a peaceful island community where he could unleash Benchley's beast. In preparation for his scouting, then, Alves gathered an armful of maps and nautical charts to best assess each site he'd visit. He needed a picturesque location, yes, but it also needed to be technically suitable, too.

Bob Mattey had concluded that a submersible platform would be needed, that having a massive control arm that could slide along a track, which would be attached to the underside of the mechanical shark. The platform that would rest on a flat seabed, one that would be only about twenty-five feet below the water's surface, and it had to be in an area where there weren't substantial tide changes – the less the better. Too high of a tide and the shark couldn't break the surface of the water but if the tide receded too much it would expose the control mechanisms. Whatever location Alves might suggest as Amity, it had to deliver what the writer envisioned, what the director would agree to, and what Mattey and his team required. It would be a tight needle to thread but that's the production designer's job.

As Benchley outlined in his novel and script treatments, Amity Island was an east coast locale; that was clear. To remain faithful to Benchley's work, then, Alves would need to travel eastward to find the sunny vacation spot the author described, all the while being attentive to his own design instincts that would refine the setting to best suit cinematic impact and believability. Trouble was, in December the east coast was anything but sunny, so Alves would have to brave the biting cold and use his insight and imagination to see past the layers of snow and disregard the frigid climate – this was going to be a summertime outing!

His first step was to dine with Benchley himself to understand the locales that had originally inspired the author. Benchley explained that Amity was an amalgam of several places he had visited while preparing his novel – the idyllic villages and townships of Montauk, Sag Harbor, and Covington, all in New York, plus Stonington in Connecticut.

THIS SPREAD / Welcome to Amity. We hope you'll enjoy your stay.

NEXT SPREAD / Despite the snow-covered landscape, Joe Alves discovers a perfect summertime setting to terrorize (left). Alves scouts JAWS on a nineteen-cent pocket notebook (right). Scouting Martha's Vineyard, Alves deems the Oaks Bluff cottages as too 'gingerbread-y' (center).

Pointing to his notes, Alves also inquired, "and this little island – Martha's Vineyard?" "Oh, I don't think there's anything there," Benchley dismissed.

Alves set off to first scout the New York locations – and they seemed nice but just not overly notable. From a design eye, he knew what he was looking for, either already established or easily (and affordably) amenable to construction. So he continued his search, now traveling by ferry, to scout Nantucket Island. An aggressive snow storm, however, turned the ferry back; the skipper said, "not today, folks." Upon return to dock, Alves noticed another ferry, apparently unimpeded, bound for Martha's Vineyard. Despite Benchley's apparent disinterest in it, Alves boarded that ferry anyway.

Upon arrival at the island, Alves checked into the Mansion House Inn to settle for the evening. The next day, with his collection of maps and tide charts, plus some island brochures he gathered from the inn, he set off to explore.

"I started in Oak Bluff; it was very nice and quaint and cute – really, a little too cute and gingerbread-y for what I thought we needed. So I traveled on to nearby Edgartown; it was practically perfect with its white picket fences, nicely lined-up houses, all sporting the right kind of Georgian styling. And, I saw that, in the short stretch between Oak Bluff and Edgartown, there was a big bay with a nice long beach; it was covered with snow at the time but I could see it would give me plenty of sandy shore to work with. Checking the maps, I saw that the depth in that bay was only twenty-five feet and the tide shift was only two feet. This was great; this is exactly what Mattey said we needed.

DISCOVERING AMITY ISLAND

95

SCOUTING NOTES & PHOTOS

THURS
11:30 AM
LONG ISLAND

Amityville about 1½ hours from Manhattan - large main street average looking town - not to much charm med. size

Babylon 12:00 TH.
Robert moses causeway - water to shallow - can see shore shooting towards island - houses on beach ocean front small.
Town sign start w/
❤ Village of

BELLPORT 12:50 THUR.
nice little town good scale eastern looking (see PHOTOS no - Hotel - a theater

Very good no beach houses

BELLPORT - GOOD LITTLE TOWN

W. ESTHAMPTON. GOOD TOWN
BEACH - THEATER
NO - HOTEL

SOUTHAMPTON - GREAT HOTEL
& BEACH HOUSES

EAST HAMPTON - LARGE TOWN -
SOME STREETS GOOD

――― NEXT DAY FR. ―――

PROMISED LAND
A GROUP OF SMALL SHACKEY HOUSES - NO HARBOR - MOST HOUSE GROUP TOGETHER

V. CHART BLOCK Is.
1211

SAG. HARBOR

GREAT LITTLE TOWN - OLD WHALING TOWN - CHARMIC HAS MOST EVERYTHING

GREENPORT - NICE TOWN LARGE HARBOR - NOT AS GOOD AS SAG HARBOR

Shooting from Horton beach - don't see land aross

――― SAT. 8 ―――

STONINGTON - very New England looking - coloum architecture - but very narrow streets hard to shoot -

ABOVE / Oak Bluff a bit too "gingerbread-y" (left) but Menemsha would be perfect to launch the sea hunt (middle and right).

— MONDAY — .
OAK BLUFF — GOOD
has most everything — good
calm ocean in area —
Nantucket sound or Vineyard
looks good — 28 ft calm
water — a good 180°

EDGARTOWN — lot of
lap sided white house — look
typical New England — very
clean looking town about
the cleanest yet — could work
very well

KATAMA SO. BEACH
LONG beach rough water
lot of bunch grass

GAY HEAD lighthouse
red brick

MENEMSHA — FISHING
VILLAGE — very quaint but
wrong for our picture — they
make lobster traps there
(maybe good for Quint place

talk with a guy at woods
Hole oceanographic Institute
— maybe we could use there
Sub — he says weather good
April - May —

————— . —————
TUESDAY
Head for Nantucket — raining
and cold —

Siasconcet very small
town — shingle house —
no real town just Post Office
general store

SANKATY HEAD
red stripe & white lighthouse
— lot of shingle house on
hill above beach

Wauwinet — no town
just a group of houses
and one hotel — not open

MADAKET NO
TOWN — JUST LITTLE
WHARF — HOUSE — SMALL
shingles — WED — . —
Nantucket — fantastic —
the most charming town I've
ever seen — but wrong for the film
couple stone streets — It look like
Disneyland — The island is to
different to work on and get to.

ABOVE / More photos of a snowy Menemsha.

Then I went on to the fishing village of Menemsha, and that really knocked me out. It had a perfect inlet and there was a perfectly-situated empty lot where I could build Quint's shack. It immediately struck me that this setting looked like something David Lean (director of *The Bridge on the River Kwai* and *Dr. Zhivago*) would have had built for one of his pictures. I really admired the look of his films but had heard the stories of the troubles he had on location for *Lawrence of Arabia*. On that one, he had to return to the studio and build sets where he could maintain better control. But, looking at these locations on Martha's Vineyard, it was all quite contained, all in close proximity, and seemingly manageable."

As much as Martha's Vineyard appeared to be tailor-made to serve as Amity, it still required a certain amount of 'dressing.' Alves would need to design and construct the proper beachfront elements as he had noted during his script breakdown – lifeguard towers, dressing cabanas, a boardwalk, and a grandstand, all along the sands of Oak Bluffs' State Beach.

Within the town proper of Edgartown, Alves found that the streets were quaintly narrow and nicely appointed in their own right; they would require only minor dressing to present them as Amity establishments: a bit of signage here, some redressed storefronts there, and quick repurposing of quiet alleyways would complete the transformation.

Remembering the needs of practicality for the location – any location – Alves ensured there would also be suitable amenities to house on-site cast and crew. Again, the Vineyard had that and all within close proximity of the various shooting locations he would recommend. The stately Pease House, in particular, seemed perfectly suited to serve as the on-island production office.

Excited by all he'd seen, Alves spotted a phone booth where he could make a call back to Universal to tell Bill Gilmore and Steven Spielberg of his discoveries. All sounded fine although Spielberg also urged a look at Marblehead in Massachusetts. Alves complied, making his way to the location. It was nice, indeed, but its tide variances were problematic.

He continued to scout all the way up to Maine, wanting to complete a full reconnaissance, taking photos of it all before returning to California. After a week's time away, Alves returned to Universal, excited to share his collection of Instamatic photos with the team. "Myself, I was very sold on the island," Alves explains, "both for its aesthetics as well as its practical features – especially that level, shallow

seabed. And when the New Year arrived, I returned to the east coast, this time with Bill and Steven. We ventured up to Marblehead so Steven could see it for himself. He agreed it was nice but, admittedly, the tides could be a problem. So then we went to Martha's Vineyard. Both of them quickly agreed it would be perfect."

Alves' quick-yet-thorough scouting had seemed to pay off and now it would be Gilmore's job, as production executive, to lay the groundwork for getting proper permissions and the buy-in from the local officials to make a movie in their quiet little hamlet. Gilmore assigned Jim Fargo as production manager; he had previously worked as assistant director on Spielberg's *Sugarland Express* and his much-lauded made-for-TV nail biter, *Duel*. Fargo would be tasked with schmoozing the island council members, the business owners, and the residents, courting and cajoling each of them in order to secure the needed local facilities and, most important, the community's cooperation. As Fargo would discover, there were several communities on the tiny island and not all were equally cooperative, especially with one another.

LEFT / Scouting the docks of Menemsha plus finding a perfect boathouse to set up the art department (bottom image).

BELOW / The local Kelly House becomes *JAWS* production headquarters, as deftly negotiated by Alves and the production team

"...we were hurrying to shoot our beach scenes while we still had the beaches to ourselves..."
BILL GILMORE, PRODUCTION EXECUTIVE

THIS SPREAD / Joe Alves' design details that transform Martha's Vineyard into sunny Amity Island.

QUINT'S SHACK

WHILE GILMORE AND FARGO WORKED to convince and appease the locals, Alves turned his thoughts back to the vacant lot where he'd erect Quint's towering shack. He built a scale model to guide him in his design while demonstrating to others how it would suit the production. He fashioned it in near-identical style and structure of the existing buildings in the area, namely Edgartown's long-standing Old Sculpin Gallery, formerly a boat shack owned by Vineyard boat builder, Manuel Swartz. "I showed my model to Bill, Steven, and others and they agreed, giving me approval to fund the construction. Getting that same approval from the Vineyard selectmen was another matter."

Having earmarked the empty waterside lot in Menemsha and having since gained approval from the property owner to build a temporary structure, Alves was ready to drive piles and cut lumber. The local selectmen, however, refused to grant a building permit, objecting that Alves' design was "too tall and exceeded local building statutes." Constructing Quint's shack would prove to be as challenging an endeavor as an encounter with the cantankerous character himself. The selectmen, pleasant though they were, had serious reservations over allowing a disruptive Hollywood movie company to run roughshod over their elite enclave. Plus, the thought of a moviemaking endeavor that would surely bring all manner of media attention was practically abhorrent; the area was still managing the impact of the not-too-long-ago Chappaquiddick affair (which made producer Zanuck, himself, uneasy). But the blue-collar locals gladly welcomed the prospect; it could mean an infusion of income and even a new source of employment for many of the local tradesmen. There was an economic chasm here, no doubt. Yes, this was a real-life socio-political schism that Benchley plainly applied to his fictitious Amity.

Alves was directed to take his case to the State House of Boston and maybe he'd gain the permits and approvals he needed to build the shack. With his scale model and his blueprints, Alves made his pitch to a State House session. Begrudgingly, approval was granted but only on the condition that he and his team agreed to restore the lot to its original condition – that meant complete removal of the structure after filming and precise restoration of the lot – dirt, debris, and all.

"Agreed."

Oh, and the posting of a lofty $500,000 bond, just to be sure the movie company would remain true to its word.

[Sigh] "Yes, agreed."

The 'shack' – a misnomer if ever there was one – would arise as a work of art, fitting seamlessly alongside the existing buildings, executed perfectly by Alves' builder, Jimmy Woods, and painter, Ward Welton.

THIS SPREAD / Joe Alves' model for Quint's shack and intended Menemsha location for construction (inset).

NEXT SPREAD / Elevation detail of Quint's shack.

Quint shack

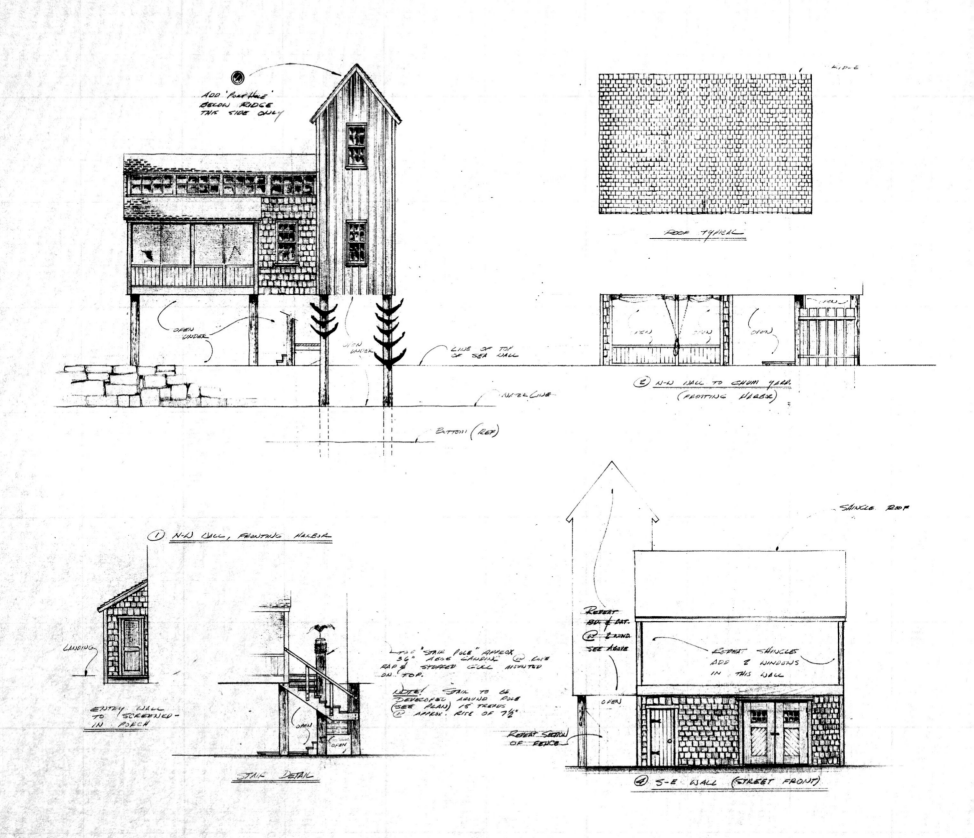

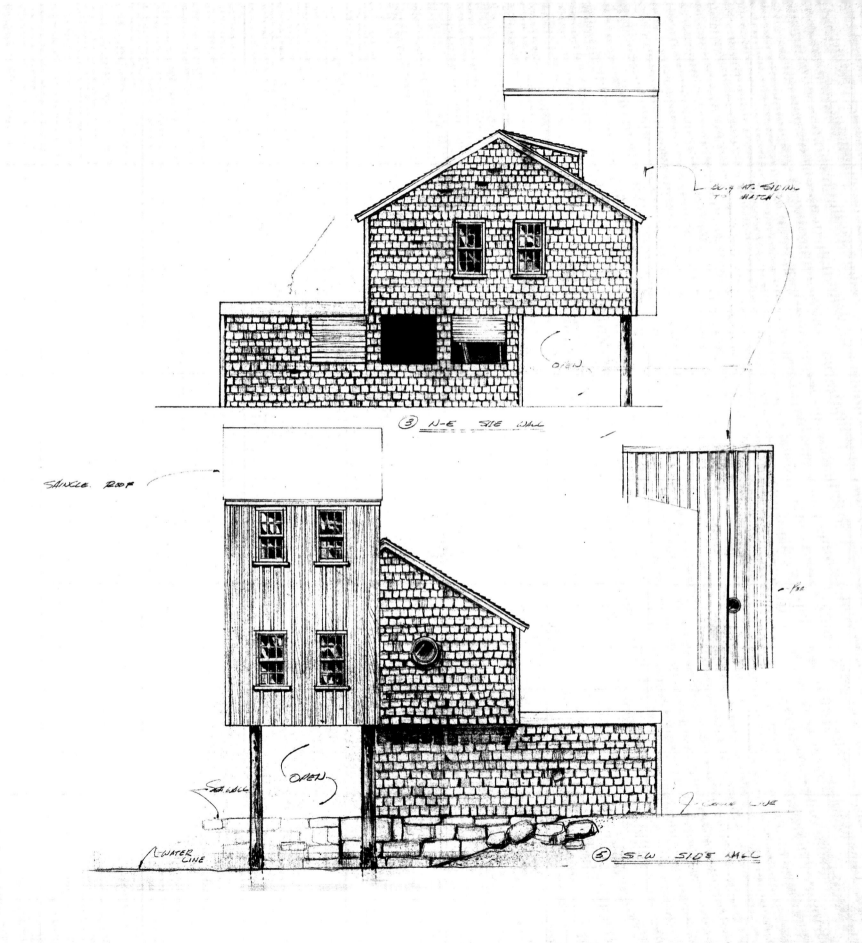

③ N-E SIDE WALL

⑤ S-W SIDE WALL

SHINGLE ROOF

WATER LINE

OPEN

SEA WALL

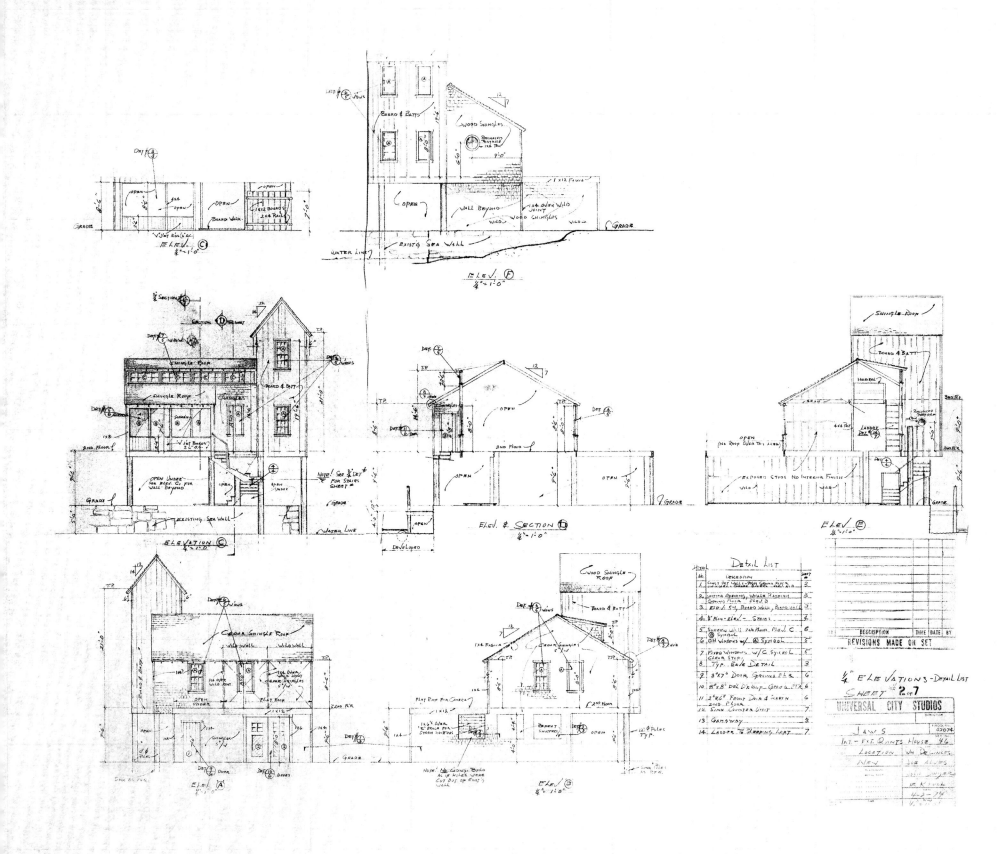

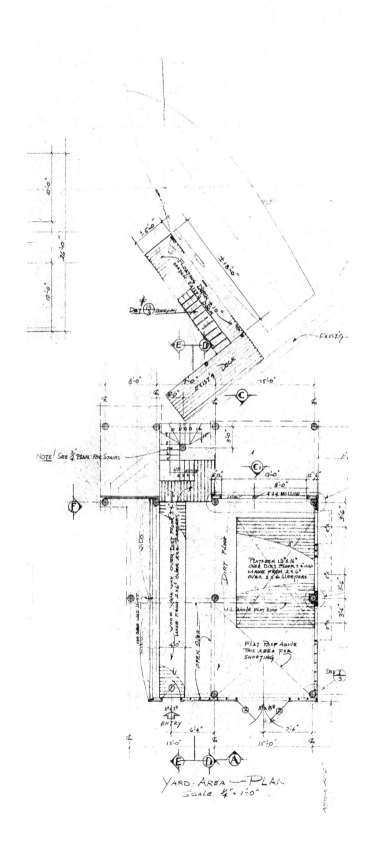

THIS SPREAD / Frank Wurmser's technical
drawing (left). In-progress and completed
photos of Quint's shack (above).

From the outset, Alves determined he'd bring along the same team members he'd worked with on *The Sugarland Express*, Woods and Welton. Both excelled in their expertise and fully understood Alves' design approach, whether it be over matters of construction style, color choices, or anything in between. They had proven themselves to be inventive, resourceful, and willing to see the job through. *JAWS*, regarded as a low-budget endeavor, comparatively speaking, would need to make do with a small 'art department.' Given that, this resourceful crew of two knew they'd be stretched paper thin on the Vineyard and so they reached out to the local Vineyard craftsmen with intention to hire whatever carpenters and artisans that might be available. As it would turn out, there weren't many seasoned builders available for hire though there were plenty of young guys willing to become overnight apprentices. Woods gathered a team of could-be builders and

quickly trained them in the craft of building movie sets and structures. Likewise, Welton found some extra hands to help him with the painting chores, with one local fellow, Kevin Pike, taking particular interest in the methods of weathering technique.

Alves, meanwhile, called in John Dwyer, a towering six-foot-five-inch fellow, to join the crew as set decorator. Dwyer was a long-time set dresser and prop handler who had worked with Alves in previous MCA and Universal productions including episodes of *McHale's Navy*, *Night Gallery*, and *Hec Ramsey*. "John Dwyer dressed the shack perfectly," Alves beamed. "He brought in lots of shark jaws, including the original set loaned to me from the Steinhart Aquarium, plus big fishing tackle and plenty of nautical stuff. He even tacked up nudie pinups on the walls. It was entirely convincing and completely looked like the sort of place where a character like Quint would live."

THIS SPREAD / The new Quint shack merged seamlessly with the other structures along the Menemsha waters (below) and dressed impeccably by John Dwyer (pictured with Joe Alves, right).

THE ORCA

AND THEN WOULD COME Quint's sharking vessel, the *Orca*. Alves knew he'd likely have to refashion an existing craft in order to get the sort of 'character' that he and director Spielberg wanted, and it was in Boston where he spotted a recently-retired lobster boat, the *Warlock*.

The *Warlock* was definitely large enough to accommodate the actors, film crew, and film equipment but it was much too sleek to suit Quint's sun-parched persona. Its best quality, however, was that it was for sale.

Bought and paid for, the *Warlock* was transported back to the boathouse workshop the team had set up at the Vineyard. Now began the task of transforming this sleek cruiser into the ruddy *Orca*. It required just about everything above the hull be removed and replaced, refitting it with oversized cabin windows (Spielberg wanted to see a perpetual surrounding of water during every cabin interior scene), a towering mast with crow's nest, and an extended pulpit jutting from its bow. Alves drew up the specifications, handing those off to the increasingly-overworked Woods. Ward Welton, similarly stretched to his limits, was tasked with painting the vessel, giving it a sinister black and burgundy color scheme – angry, aged, and cruelly authoritarian, reflecting Quint's own despotic persona.

***THIS SPREAD** / The Warlock, a lobster boat soon to be transformed into sharking vessel, the Orca.*

LEFT / Joe Alves begins plotting the rebuilding of the *Warlock* into the *Orca*

BELOW / Alves on-island art department charts the transformation of a lobster boat into a sharker's vessel.

And here's the importance of color to a film's designer. The designer is responsible for interpreting the film's script, its characters' personalities, and its director's vision, using that information to determine which colors will support the agreed-upon design. In this regard, this collaboration determines, literally, which colors will be seen on screen... and, oftentimes, which ones won't.

For *JAWS*, Martha's Vineyard presented a color palette of its own – tones, hues, and temperatures – that offered the look (that is, the mood) that both Alves and Spielberg agreed it needed. Shades of white, gray, and pale blue were prevalent around the island, all of it with a somewhat muted look after seasons of exposure to sun, sand, and salt. This subdued palette already on display offered plenty of opportunity to provide stark contrasts to dramatically reinforce the juxtaposition of a sleepy township that's unexpectedly terrorized by

a giant predator. The *JAWS* palette, then, would be simple but effective. Alves would then generously incorporate the use of yellow, given it is a natural contrast to blue.

Red would be for blood – and that's all. Spielberg was adamant that red be completely absent from the production design save for the on-screen carnage. Alves agreed. Therefore, the *Orca* was painted in shades of burgundy, not red. The beachside cabanas were painted with dark orange stripes; again, not red. Alves saw to it that none of his designs incorporated the deliberate use of red, making sure his team understood the directive, too.

Back to the transformation of the Warlock, Alves instructed that his team would actually build two ships, the *Orca* and the *Orca II*, the second of which would serve as a duplicate rigged to be sunk and resurfaced as needed for filming of the climactic ending sequences.

ABOVE / Behold the *Orca*, finely rebuilt and expertly weathered by Alves' art department.

PETER BENCHLEY'S NOVEL WAS released in February 1974, about the same time that the Magnificent Seven were busy building the shark and while Alves was crisscrossing the country to ready the filming location. *JAWS*, the novel, became a runaway bestseller, taking all by surprise. Gleefully, publisher Doubleday quickly readied a paperback edition under its imprint, Bantam Books. Readers across the nation and soon across the globe were swallowing *JAWS* whole. A most adamant review insisted, "Read *JAWS* – by all means, read it!" The public complied.

Zanuck, Brown, and the executives at Universal knew they needed to get their picture out quickly while interest in the novel was peaking. And so it was in March of 1974 when the producers made their entreaty:

"Can you start filming in April?"

"But I don't even have a script yet," complained Spielberg.

"And the sharks aren't finished yet," added Alves, "and Gilmore and Fargo are still working to get the rest of the permits we need to complete the sets."

After some hem-hawing and heel digging by Spielberg, unafraid to confront his bosses for their audacious request, the principal photography start date was pushed out to May 2. OK – that's a bit better than April but, hey, there was still so much to get done.

"There were times early in the picture when we felt we had made a mistake," Brown later confided, "because Steven was maddeningly perfectionistic... and our gifted production designer, Joe Alves, was so meticulous in seeking expert counsel [on development of the sharks]." To Alves' consternation, all had forgotten that developing the shark was decreed to be a one- to two-year endeavor; Punky Chinque said it, the guys at Disney said it, and Joe Lombardi said it. And even when Bob Mattey said, "We can do anything," Alves never interpreted that to mean "anything, by tomorrow." Nothing remained to be said except, "All hands on deck!"

LEFT / Filming the scene: below the surface, the shark attacks Hooper's cage as actors Roy Scheider (left) and Robert Shaw struggle to rescue him.

BELOW / Actor Richard Dreyfuss, producer David Brown, and director Steven Spielberg (left). Joe Alves watches filming from atop the navigation deck (middle). Filming the scene: "Dammit Martin! You screw around with these tanks and they're gonna blow up!" (right).

Bob Mattey responded to the schedule pull-up with his unflappable good spirit. "Well, let's get to it," he cheerily answered back to Alves. By this point, the full-length twenty-five-foot shark was propped up in the middle of the Sunland workspace, flanked by the other two half-sharks, all surrounded by numerous work tables, equipment, and busy people. The Magnificent Seven had grown some, bringing on a few more hired guns: WDI sculptors Joe Kaba and Peter Kermode were brought in to assist Don Chandler, plus additional welder Bill Shourt was enlisted. Stan Mahoney had been ably serving as shop foreman, keeping all the activities aligned and moving forward while ensuring the team had everything it needed to build the giant sharks. Mattey, though, was still operating as Alves' go-to guy, reassuring that the shark would "perform" when director Spielberg would shout "Action!"

He practically guaranteed it.

And so Alves hurried along his Magnificent Seven while hiring on even more Vineyard locals to complete set construction and all else necessary to get the production camera-ready.

And while he – and everyone else – waited with baited breath to hear when the sharks might be arriving, director Spielberg shot as much of the non-shark scenes as possible.

It was in April that Mattey indicated that the sharks were working in dry tests. According to Alves, "it wiggled a bit." Mattey was confident it would work as needed when lowered into the ocean. So when word of the wiggling reached Bill Gilmore and then David Brown, the producer quickly dispatched a congratulatory telegram to Alves:

```
FINAL SHARK DEMONSTRATION FANTASTIC SUCCESS.  MOST
SINCERE CONGRATULATIONS TO YOU AND MATTEY. SEE YOU
MONDAY. DICK AND BILL.
```

Alves knew that any protest he offered in request of more time to 'wet test' the sharks would be denied. In this business, time and budget always trumped art and assurance. As a production designer, he'd have to make do with what he was given, then stretch to make the very best of what he and his team would deliver (and they would).

The sharks traveled by tractor-trailer across the U.S., unfortunately arriving damaged after they somehow broke loose of their shipping frames. Mattey and the Magnificent Seven had set up an on-site 'Shark City' workshop at the local Norton & Easterbrook boathouse where they proceeded to repair and ready the sharks.

And during the time that the sharks weren't exactly ready, neither was the shooting script. Benchley handed it off to Spielberg indicating he'd done all he could do with it. Spielberg then handed it over to his good friend, writer/actor Carl Gottlieb, asking that he flesh out the characters and add some punch and levity to the proceedings.

Final touches to the sharks included the painting of the skin, Alves choosing the same color as film editor Verna Fields' KEM editing console. "KEM Gray," he would call it. Ward Welton matched the color, then added #40 silica sand to the mixture to give the shark skin realistic texture. And so it seemed that the sharks were ready for filming. Or maybe not…

What the team hadn't expected was the perpetual electrolysis of the salt water, which quickly ate away at the sharks' intricate interior mechanisms. That, plus the relentless wave action and water pressure of the open ocean that knocked the sharks silly. But Mattey never gave in and never let his team give up. "It'll look better in the morning," he'd tell his his team. "We'll get it fixed and try again."

Ultimately, the sharks began working well, their performances improving with each day as Mattey and team learned how to manage them in the unforgiving waters. Knowing now what the sharks could and couldn't do, Alves worked with Spielberg to draw up storyboards that would define the film's climactic third act.

LEFT / Bob Mattey, always ready to take on the task, by land or sea or foam…

BELOW / Previously shrouded in secrecy, the shark is ready to make its big debut.

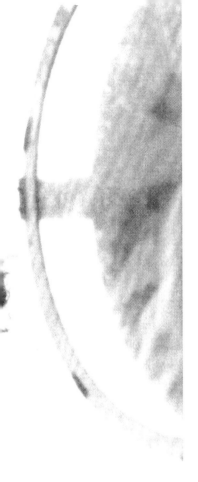
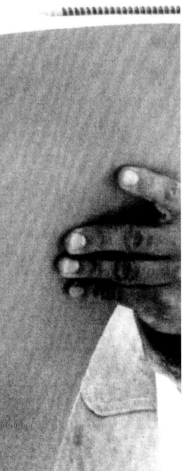

THE STORYBOARDS

IN FILMMAKING, STORYBOARDS ARE indispensible roadmaps for what will be filmed. The storyboard captures an agreed-upon view for a scene to be shot, usually through conference between a film's production designer, director, photographer, and possibly technicians responsible for complex effects. Joe Alves would serve as the conduit between the effects team (understanding from Mattey what the sharks could do and couldn't do, and how they could and should be filmed) and director Spielberg.

So while the script continued to evolve under Carl Gottlieb's steady hand and Mattey and his team labored to get the sharks to behave for the director, Spielberg spent his time shooting as much of the non-shark sequences as possible. Again, as the script was in perpetual flux, Spielberg would often improvise while shooting, electing for different angles or dialog changes, easy with much of the walk-and-talk sequences. But when it came to filming with the shark, there was no such improvisation.

With the third act of the picture – where the principals are aboard the *Orca* while the shark eyed them as potential snacks – the script had practically been set aside. Spielberg would tell Alves what he wanted to capture while Alves rendered storyboards of what the director described – this usually took place during their daily lunch, often while perched upon the *Orca's* pulpit.

They'd agree on the angle and the direction of the shot so Alves could specify which shark would be needed. Since it took an entire morning to tug the shark into the water, set the platform, set the effects barge, and set the camera platform, there was no opportunity for improvisation.

Copies of the storyboards were then tacked up on the wall in the production office, serving as an illustrated agenda for each day's shoot (Alves always kept his binder of the originals with him every day of the shoot). Richard Zanuck, who had been spending considerable time on the island to monitor the company's progress, took special pleasure in marking a red 'X' on each storyboard as the footage was captured and completed.

But it wasn't only the sharks that required precise storyboarding and pre-planning; the seemingly innocuous yellow barrels that were tethered to the harpooned shark needed the same considerations. Alves and Spielberg would agree on the direction of the shoot, the position of the horizon line, and the weather conditions (because the alternating clear skies, cloudy skies were already proving a challenge for editor Verna Fields, who would struggle to match the cumulus from scene to scene).

Alves sketched the storyboard compositions on thick-stock paper, first in pencil, then he detailed them over with pen and ink. As a final touch, he added shadows and mid-tones using thinned India ink, applied with a brush, to suggest the lighting levels that Spielberg specified. He cut out each of the scenes and glued them, three up, onto hole-punched sheets of 8½" x 11" card stock, keeping them all secured within his sturdy three-ring binder.

THIS SPREAD / Joe Alves sketches a scene treatment for director Spielberg (center) and producer Richard D. Zanuck (far left).

HOOPER'S NIGHT DIVE

108A LONG SHOT BOAT MOVING
LIGHT HOUSE IN BACKGROUND

108B CAMERA MOVES IN ON
FASCINATIN - RHYTHM - NOTE !
(COLORED LIGHTS IN THE COCKPIT)

108C CAMERA STILL MOVING IN
UNTIL WE ARE CLOSE ON HOOPER
AND BRODY

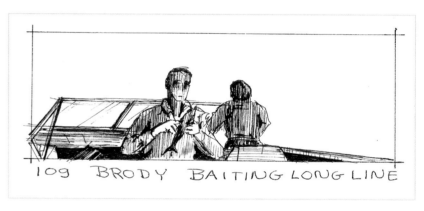

109 BRODY BAITING LONG LINE

110 BRODY - HOOPER - MOVE IN
TOWARD FATHOMETER

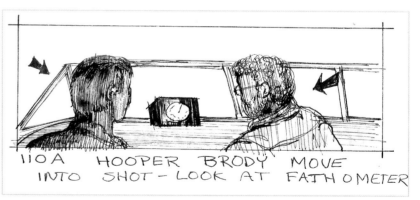

110A HOOPER BRODY MOVE
INTO SHOT - LOOK AT FATHOMETER

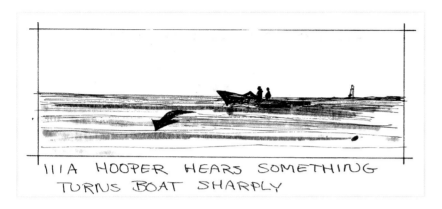

111A HOOPER HEARS SOMETHING TURNS BOAT SHARPLY

111B BOAT COMES TOWARDS US

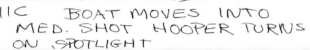

111C BOAT MOVES INTO MED. SHOT HOOPER TURNS ON SPOTLIGHT

111D SPOTLIGHT IN LENS WE FADED TO WHITE

112 WATER LEVEL AT BOW — CUTTING THRU DEBRIS — FLICKA IN THE BACKGROUND

113 CLOSE ON BROKEN CLEAT OF THE FLICKA — SPOTLIGHT IN BACKGROUND

114 CLOSE ON DEBRIS-SPOT-
LIGHT MOVING AROUND

114A OVER HOOPER-FINDING
THE FLICKA

115 CLOSE ON BRODY-GREEN
SONAR LIGHT ON HIS FACE

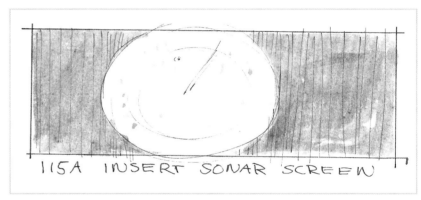

115A INSERT SONAR SCREEN

116 HOOPER WITH FLASH LIGHT
LOOKING UNDERWATER

116A HOOPER GOE'S BELOW-BRODY
STANDING ALONE

117a SHOOTING FROM CABIN

117b HOOPER WALK INTO SHOT

117C HOOPER TELLS BRODY HE'S GOING IN THE WATER

117 A1 ON HOOPER'S BACK – HE GOES INTO THE WATER

117 A2 SAME ANGLE BRODY STANDING THERE ALONE

120 A1 HOOPER EMERGING FROM THE WATER – GASPING FOR BREATH

120 A2 BRODY HELPING HOOPER CLIMB INTO BOAT

120 A3 HOOPER "JESUS CHRIST! A GREAT WHITE"

ACT III STORYBOARDS

179
180 QUINT - BRODY - LOOKING HARD
(DUSK)

180a SHARK IS SEEN FOR FIRST TIME
(D) (L.TOR. PLATF. SHARK)

181 OVER HOOPER - SEEING SHARK TURN
TO PORT SIDE (DUSK)
(SEA SLED SHARK)

182 HOOPER COMES DOWN -
SHARK MOVES ON PORT SIDE - AT AN ANGLE
183 AWAY FROM ORCA (DUSK) (SEA SLED SHARK)

183A¹ HOOPER IN PILOT HOUSE SHARK
MOVING AWAY - THRU WINDOW
(SEA SLED SHARK)

183A² QUINT RIGGING GUN - HOOPER
RUNS OUT WITH CAMERA - BRODY
PASSES BY OUTSIDE - SHARK MOVING AWAY
(SEA SLED SHARK)

183 A3 HOOPER TELLS BRODYS TO
GET ON THE PULPIT · SHARK MOVING
ACROSS BOW   (SEA SLED SHARK)

183 A4 OVER HOOPER · SHOOTING
BRODY · SHARK PASSES BY· TURNS
OUT TO HIS LEFT.   (SEA SLED SHARK)

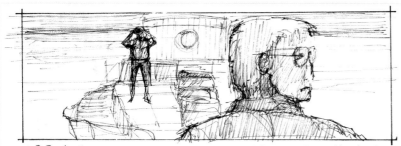

183 A5 C.U. BRODY · LOOKING BACK AT
SHARK · HOOPER ·WITH CAMERA
                (·SEAS

183 B QUINT APPEARS WITH HARPOON
GUN

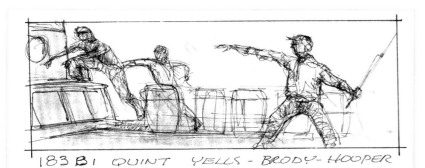

183 B1 QUINT YELLS · BRODY · HOOPER
MOVE ·

183 B2 OVER BRODY · QUINT ·
              (ON BRIDGE)   (ON PULPIT)
SHARK HEADING TOWARDS BOW
(IN DISTANCE)   (SEA SLED SHARK)

183 B3   P.O.V. QUINT OF HOOPER
IN PILOT HOUSE

183 C   CLOSE ON HOOPER FINDING
STROBE   SHARK OUTSIDE WINDOW

183 C1   HOOPER CLIMBS OUT THRU
WINDOW

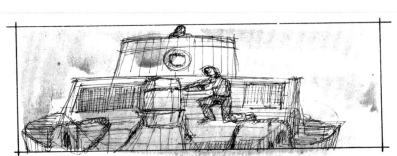

183 D.   BRODY ON BRIDGE - HOOPER
RIGGING BARRELS

183 E   CLOSE ON QUINT
(SEA SLED SHARK)

183 E1   CLOSE ON BOW OF ORCA
SHARK COMING CLOSE
(L.TO.R. PLATE SHARK)

183 E 2 (FROM CROWS NEST) QUINT FIRES HARP. (L. TO R. PLATF. SHARK)

183 E 3 WATER EXPLODES - WITH SHARK TAIL (L. TO. R PLATF. SHARK)

183 E 4 QUINT GETS SPLASHED

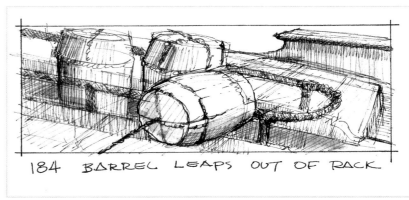

184 BARREL LEAPS OUT OF RACK

184 A BARREL POPS OVER BOARD

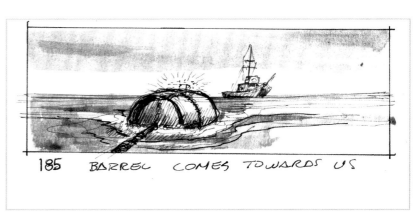

185 BARREL COMES TOWARDS US

186 A1 HOPPER JUMPS ON FLYING BRIDGE

186 A2 HOPPER GRABS WHEEL TURNS BOAT FOLLOWS BARREL

186 A3 HOOPER - BRODY - FOLLOWING BARREL - BARREL DISAPPEARS

186 A4 BARREL DISAPPEARS ORCA MOVES IN CLOSE

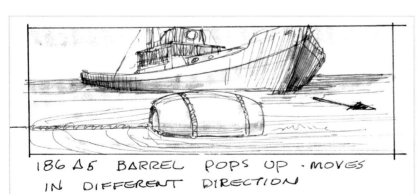

186 A5 BARREL POPS UP - MOVES IN DIFFERENT DIRECTION

186 A6 ORCA TURNS HARD - AFTER BARREL

186A7 QUINT ON PULPIT LOOKING AT HOOPER

186A8 HOOPER ON BRIDGE LOOKING AT QUINT

187 ORCA OPEN SEA NIGHT STROBE ON BARREL

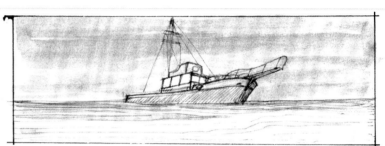

191A EXT. ORCA (DAY FOR NIGHT) (HOT LIGHTS IN ORCA)

193 BARREL MOVES IN RIGHT TO LEFT STROBE BLINKING (HOT LIGHTS IN ORCA) (DAY FOR NIGHT)

195a1 QUINT MOVES OUT FROM PILOT HOUSE—STARTS SHOOTING AHEAD OF BARREL

195a2 QUINT SHOOTING — CLOSE
ON BARREL AND STROBE

195a3 QUINT MOVES INTO C.U.
STROBE LIGHT BRIGHT ON HIS FACE
(D.FORN)

195b QUINT—"CUT ENGINE"—BRODY GET
UP FRONT " (D FORN)

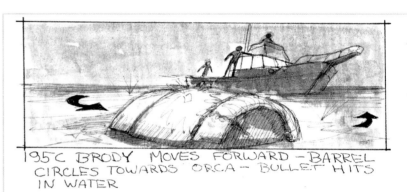

195C BRODY MOVES FORWARD — BARREL
CIRCLES TOWARDS ORCA — BULLET HITS
IN WATER

195d BRODY WALKS UP FRONT — SHARK HITS
AND   ORCA — CUT TO (195e)
195d1 CLOSE ON BAG — BRODY WALKS INTO C.U.

195d2 BRODY WALKS IN TO C.U.
HAND REACHES IN BAG — PULLS
OUT GUN.

195d₃   PAN UP WITH GUN—SEE
BRODY'S FACE MOST TERRIFIED—LIGHT
FROM STROBE ON HIS FACE/DAY-FOR
NIGHT

195e   BRODY ALMOST FALLS OVER—
BOARD (CUT BACK TO 195d)

196 MATT SHOT—BARREL CIRCLING ORCA
PHOSPHORESCENCE EFFECT—SHOOTING STARS
TO BE ANIMATED (DAY-FOR NIGHT)

197 QUINT-HOOPER, WORKING—HEADS
POP UP (D)

198 BARREL POPS UP — BRODY
POINTS TO BARREL - (D)

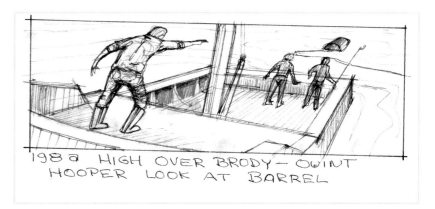

198a HIGH OVER BRODY—QUINT
HOOPER LOOK AT BARREL

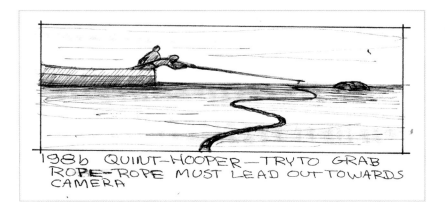

198b QUINT-HOOPER—TRY TO GRAB ROPE—ROPE MUST LEAD OUT TOWARDS CAMERA

198c CL. ON BARREL HOOPER HOOKS ROPE

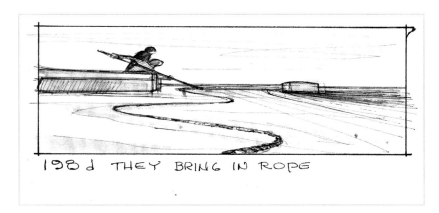

198d THEY BRING IN ROPE

198e C.U. HOOPER—QUINT "EASY JUST WANT TO GOOSE HIM UP"

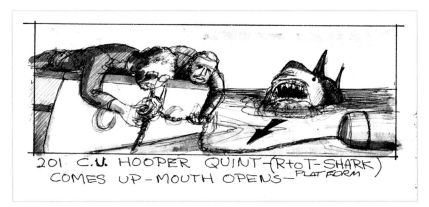

201 C.U. HOOPER QUINT—(R to T—SHARK) COMES UP—MOUTH OPENS—PLATFORM

202 BRODY YELLS—"SHARK STARBOARD"

203 C.U. HOOPER – QUINT – HEADS
TURN INTO SHOT – SHARKS P.O.V.–
HEADS JUMP BACK –

203 a / SHARK TURNS ON SIDE / ROPE
IN MOUTH – MOUTH CLOSES ON ROPE
(R. TO L. SHARK)   (R. TO L. PLATE SHARK)

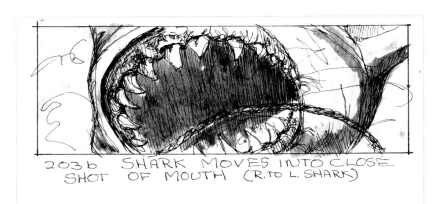

203 b   SHARK MOVES INTO CLOSE
SHOT OF MOUTH (R. TO L. SHARK)

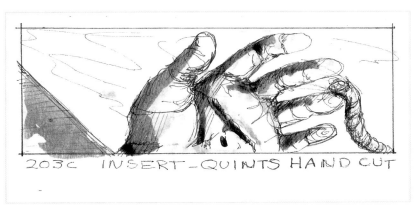

203 c   INSERT – QUINTS HAND CUT

203 d   TAIL HITS ORCA – KNOCKS OFF
"A" – WATER EXPLOSION – (R. TO L. SHARK)

203 e   PAN SHOT (L. TO R.) BRODY
MOVES WITH PAN – QUINT – HOOPER
FALL ON DECK – WATER EXPLOSION
TO MATCH (203d)

203 f END OF PAN SHOT — SEA SLED
SHARK MOVING (L. TO R.)

203 g C.U QUINT LOOKING AT CUT
HAND — HOOPER IN BACKGROUND

210 a DOLLY SHOT (210a—210d) QUINT
SAYS — "NO COMIN' RIGHT AT US"
(SEA SLED SHARK — R. TO L.)

210 b SHOOTING THRU. CABIN GLASS
QUINT RUNS UP FRONT (SEA SLED SHARK)
MOVING R. TO L. IN BACKGROUND

210 c QUINT RUNS FOR GREENER
GUN (SHARK IN BACKGROUND)

210 d QUINT GRABS GREENER GUN
(SHARK STILL IN BACKGROUND)
(NOTE GREENER GUN MOUNTED UP FRONT NEAR BARRELS)

210e (PAN 210d to 210e) QUINT RUN UP ON PULPIT

210f OVER QUINT—SHOOTS HARD INTO SHARK — (R.TO L. PLAE SHARK)

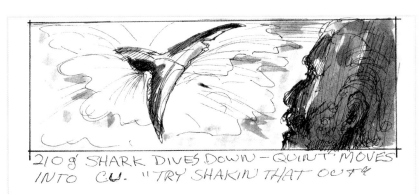

210g SHARK DIVES DOWN—QUINT MOVES INTO CU. "TRY SHAKIN THAT OUT!"

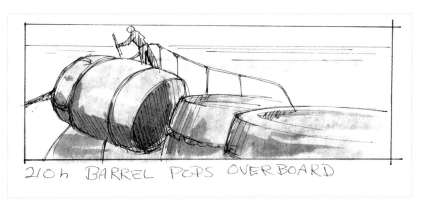

210h BARREL POPS OVERBOARD

211a BARREL IN WATER—BRODY SAYS "GET HIM IN THE HEAD"

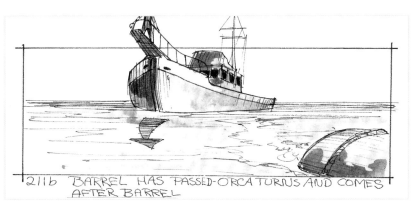

211b BARREL HAS PASSED-ORCA TURNS AND COMES AFTER BARREL

212a AT WATER LEVEL—ORCA CLOSING ON BARREL

212b OVER HOOPER ON BRIDGE—QUINT ON PULPIT—"MORE GAS GO TO HALF .ETC HOOPER—"WE CANT REV. THIS HIGH

212c₁ BARREL GOES PAST CAMERA

212c₂ SAME CAMERA POSITION ORCA GOES BY

212d INSERT ON TACK-OR-SPEED-OMETER

212e HOOPER STEERING ORCA

212 A2 BARRELS GO OFF IN THE DISTANCE AND DISAPPEAR

213a BARRELS POP UP, ORCA TURNS—(COMES INTO SHOT 213b)

213b "GRAB YOURSELFS A COUPLE OF POLES"

213c C.U. OVER QUINT "PULL IN THE ROPES AND TIE 'EM ONTO THE TRANSOM"

214a C.U. ON BRODYS HANDS—TIES ROPE ON STARBOARD CLEAT

214b ROPE TIGHTENS BRODY JUMPS BACK

212 J1 ORCA TURNS BACK - (R to L.) PLATF. SHARK BREAKS WATER - QUINT LEANS OVER PULPIT CAN'T GET A SHOT - TURNS TOWARDS US

212 J2 SHARK MOVE INTO CAMERA - QUINT SHOOTS - HARPOON COME AT US - HITS SHARK - (R. to L. PLATF. SHARK)

212 K - QUICK CUT - SHARK TURNS HEAD TOWARDS - ORCA (R. TO L PLATF. SHARK)

212 L (SEA SLED SHARK) TURNS - COMES ALONG SIDE ORCA

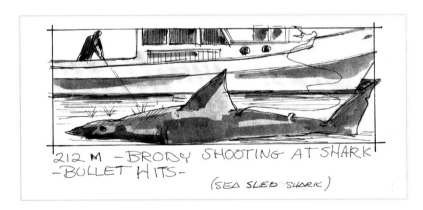

212 M - BRODY SHOOTING AT SHARK - BULLET HITS - (SEA SLED SHARK)

212 M1 BARREL POPS OVERBOARD (SEA SLED SHARK)

212 f BOAT-TO-BOAT SHOT - QUINT LOADING GREENER GUN

212 g BRODY LOADING GUN WATER HITTING NEAR STERN

212 h ORCA HITS BARREL

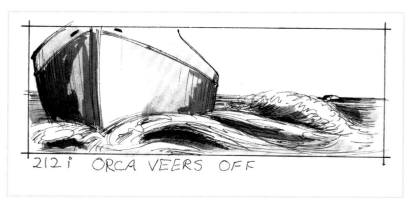

212 i ORCA VEERS OFF

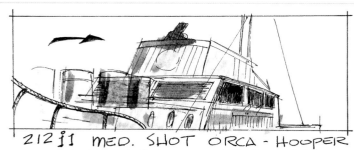

212 j1 MED. SHOT ORCA - HOOPER TURNING FAST - QUINT SWINGS INTO SHOT

212 j2 QUINT ON PULPIT - LOADING GREENER GUN - MOVE IN ON QUINT

214C HOOPER SEES ROPE-DUCKS DOWN IN TIME AS ROPE RACES OFF OF TRANSOM

215a ROPES SWING FROM PORT TO STARBOARD - STARTS DRAGGING BOAT

215b ORCA SWINGS AROUND

215c QUINT SURPRISED

215d1 ORCA BEING JERKED DOWN

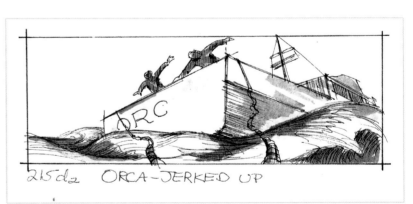

215d2 ORCA-JERKED UP

216   HOOPER - BRODY - BEING KNOCKED DOWN

217a   QUINT - "HERE'S A LITTLE FORWARD FOR YOU"

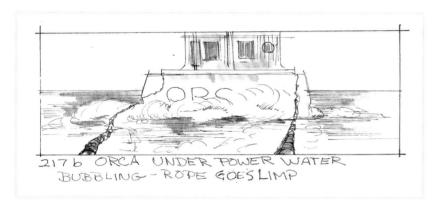

217b   ORCA UNDER POWER WATER BUBBLING - ROPE GOES LIMP

217c   QUINT TURNS TOO SEE GAIN OF POWER

217d   QUINTS P.O.V. - SHARK COMES OUT OF WATER (L. TO R. PLATE SHARK)

217e   QUINT COMES DOWN LADDER WALKS INTO C.U. (217f)

217f C.U. QUINT LOADING GREENER GUN - (PAN WITH QUINT) - (TO 217g-h)

217g QUINT CROSSES IN FRONT OF CAMERA - PAN TO 217h

217h QUINT - BRODY - HOOPER

217i (L.TOR - PLATF. SHARK) BREAKS WATER

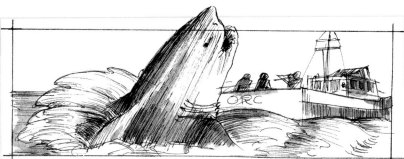

217j SHARK SLIDES BACK AS QUINT SHOOTS HITTING SHARK IN UNDERSIDE

217K BIG WATER EXPLOSION - LENS GETS WET

217L QUINT - "UNTIE US"

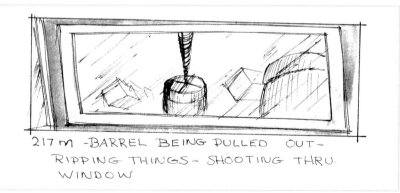

217m - BARREL BEING PULLED OUT - RIPPING THINGS - SHOOTING THRU. WINDOW

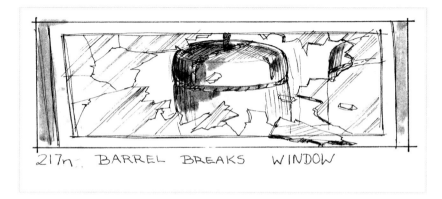

217n. BARREL BREAKS WINDOW

217 o BRODY TURNS SEES BARREL

217p BRODY JUMPS BACK AS BARREL GOES BY

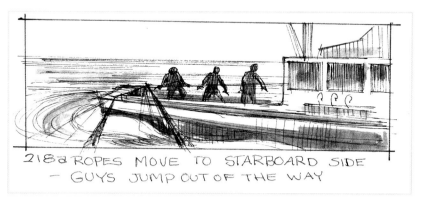

218a ROPES MOVE TO STARBOARD SIDE - GUYS JUMP OUT OF THE WAY

218b ORCA BEING SWUNG AROUND

218c ORCA BEING DRAGGED
BACKWARDS - WATER GOING INTO BOAT

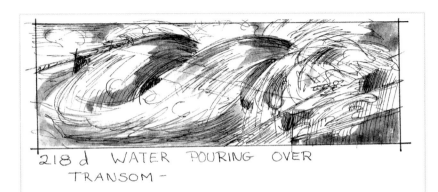

218d WATER POURING OVER
TRANSOM -

218d1 WATER GOES IN CABIN,
WASHES DOWN ENGINE HATCH
- STEAM COMES FROM ENGINE

218 e1 - SHOOTING FROM BELOW DECK,
WATER POURING INTO CABIN, DOWN
STAIRS, QUINT WALKS IN.

218 e2 QUINT WALKS INTO C.U.
GRABS KNIFE.

218f ORCA TOWED INTO SHOT—
ROPES SLACK OFF.

219a CLOSE ON CLEAT- QUINT COMES
OUT WITH KNIFE AS CLEAT
EXPLODES!

219b - QUINT TURNS TO STAR—
BOARD CLEAT.

219c CLOSE ON OTHER CLEAT—IT
EXPLODES AS WE SEE 3 BARRELS GO
OFF IN THE DISTANCE AND DISAPPEAR
UNDERWATER

219d RAKING SHOT — GUYS FALL
DOWN 1-2-3 TO THEIR KNEES

220 BARRELS POP UP 1-2-3

220 a1 — 270° PAN SHOT (220 a1 TO 220 a8)
OVER GUYS - BARRELS IN BACK-
GROUND

220 a2 BRODY STANDS UP-
BARRELS START MOVING

220 a3 PAN DOWN TO BOOTS
WE SEE WET DECK

220 a4 BRODY PICKS UP SOME-
THING

220 a5 PAN UP WITH BRODY
(BARRELS MOVING IN BACKGROUND)
QUINT LOOKING FOR PUMP

220 a6 QUINT STANDS UP - GIVES
BRODY PUMP - BARRELS MOVE
OUT OF FRAME

220 a7 BRODY TAKES PUMP
QUINT HEADS. FOR LADDER

220 a8 QUINT CLIMBING LADDER
(END OF PAN)

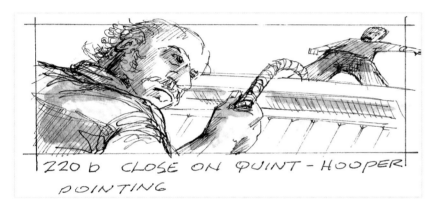

220 b CLOSE ON QUINT - HOOPER
POINTING

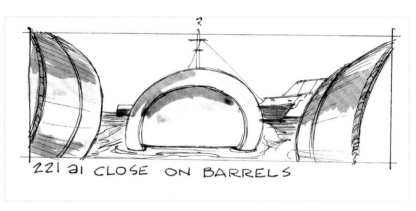

221 a1 CLOSE ON BARRELS

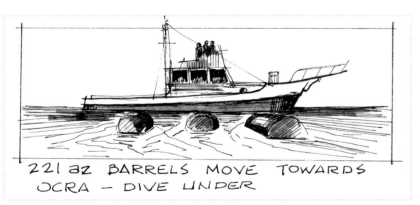

221 a2 BARRELS MOVE TOWARDS
OCRA - DIVE UNDER

221 a3 BARRELS UNDER ORCA-
BRODY "WHERE'D HE GO - QUINT " HE
CAN'T STAY DOWN, ETC. - BRODY. "HAVE
YOU EVER HAD ONE DO THIS!"

221b QUINT - "NO"

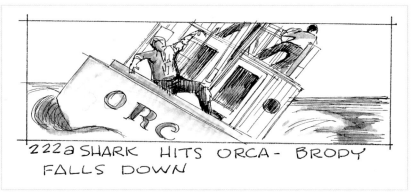

222a SHARK HITS ORCA- BRODY FALLS DOWN

222b BRODY HITS HIS HEAD

222c QUINT FALLS ON HOOPER

222d BRODY CLIMBS UP INTO SHOT - QUINT - HOOPER GETTING UP

222e MOVE IN WITH BRODY - BRODY POINTS - QUINT "FOLLOW HIM"

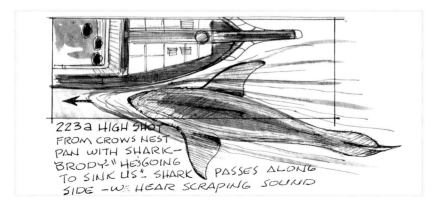

223a HIGH SHOT FROM CROWS NEST PAN WITH SHARK—BRODY:" HE'S GOING TO SINK US". SHARK PASSES ALONG SIDE —WE HEAR SCRAPING SOUND

223 b QUINT WALKS INTO CLOSE UP "DEAD ASTERN — ZIG — ZAG"

223 C1 CLOSE ON STERN — MOVE OUT TO (223 C2)

223 C2 · ORCA MOVING OUT— BLACK SMOKE STARTS COMING OUT OF EXHAUST PIPE

223 d INSERT —HOOPER ON POWER

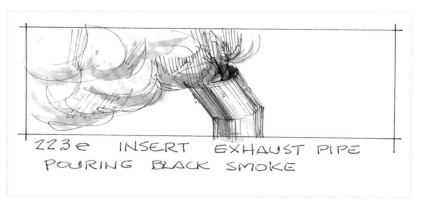

223 e INSERT EXHAUST PIPE POURING BLACK SMOKE

223f INSERT - ENGINE HATCH COVER - BLACK SMOKE COMING OUT

223g1 BARRELS GOING AWAY — TURNING AROUND

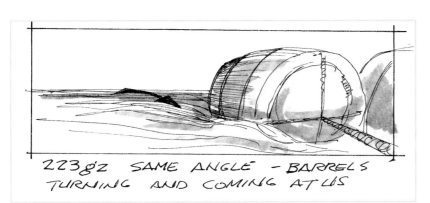

223g2 SAME ANGLE — BARRELS TURNING AND COMING AT US

223h1 ORCA GOES BY — WATER LEVEL SHOT

223h2 BARRELS CHASING ORCA

223h3 ORCA AND BARRELS GO OFF IN THE DISTANCE

223i CLOSE ON GAS LEVER - BARRELS IN BACKGROUND

223j BRODY -"HE'S CHASING US" PAN TO QUINT ⟶

223K QUINT "FULL THROTTLE TO PORT!"

223L CLOSE ON EXHAUST PIPE BLACK SMOKE POURING OUT

223m1 ORCA - PORT SIDE - LOTS OF BLACK SMOKE

223m2 SAME ANGLE - ORCA COMES IN CLOSE - SMOKE FILLS THE CABIN.

223n SHOOTING FROM INSIDE CABIN, FILLED WITH SMOKE - WE SEE THE SHARK BREAK THE WATER SURFACE.

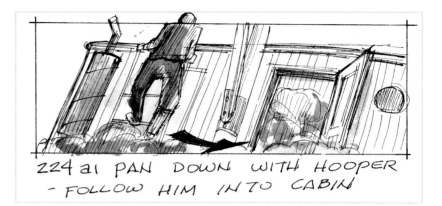

224 a1 PAN DOWN WITH HOOPER - FOLLOW HIM INTO CABIN

224 a2 HOOPER GOES IN AND DOWN TO LOWER CABIN - SMOKE THINNING OUT.

224 a3 ENGINE BLOWS UP - HATCH COVER EXPLODES.

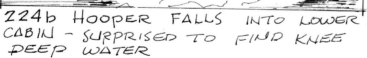

224 b HOOPER FALLS INTO LOWER CABIN - SURPRISED TO FIND KNEE DEEP WATER

224c INSERT - HOOPER GRABS GUN - LOADS IT.

224d1 OVER HOOPER - WE FOLLOW HIM OUT THE CABIN - SHARK DIVING DOWN IN THE BACKGROUND

224d2 OVER HOOPER OUT OF CABIN - SHARK DOWN - BARRELS MOVE OUT

224 e1 FULL SHOT - ORCA - BARRELS COMING TOWARDS US

224 e2 CLOSE ON BARRELS DIVING DOWN

225 ORCA - LONG SHOT - LAND IN THE BACKGROUND (NOTE! ORCA SETTING DEEP IN THE WATER)

226 a1 QUINT C.U. - LOOKING SHAKEN, DISLOCATED - "WHAT CAN YOUR GUN DO"

JOE ALVES DESIGNING JAWS

227d1 IN CABIN SHOOTING OUT—HOOPER WALKS INTO C.U., BRODY WORKING ON CAGE- QUINT LOOKING IN AT THE WINDOW

227d2 CLOSE ON HOOPER—WE SEE FEAR ON HIS FACE

227e SHOOTING FROM INSIDE THE CAGE — HOOPER ON TOP

227f1 SHOOTING FROM GIN POLE HOOPER CLIMBS IN CAGE ("TAKE ME UP")

227f.2 SAME CAMERA POSITION ON POLE CAGE SWINGS OUT OVER THE WATER AND LOWERS

227g QUINT HANDS HOOPER GUN

227h1 OVER HOOPER, GRABS GUN

227h2 HOOPER REMOVES CAP ON GUN POINT

228a CLOSE ON QUINT AT THE WINCH HOOPER IN BACK-GROUND

228b HOOPERS P.O.V GOING DOWN IN CAGE

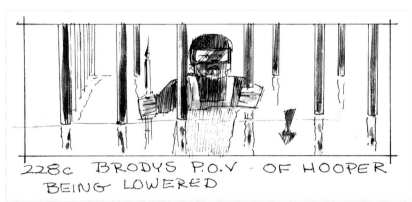

228c BRODYS P.O.V - OF HOOPER BEING LOWERED

228d CLOSE ON SHARK AS IT PASSES ORCA IN BACKGROUND

243d OVER QUINT ON WINCH – CAGE
COMES UP BENT AND TWISTED

243e CLOSE ON BENT CAGE – BRODY
"HE'S TAKEN HIM"

243f C.U. QUINT – "HE'S
COMING UP"

244a SHARK BREAKS WATER

244b SHARK CRASHES DOWN
ON TRANSOM

244c GIANT JAWS SNAPPING
AT EVERYTHING

244d OVER SHARK AT BRODY & QUINT - HANGING ON

245 BRODY - QUINT FIGHTING TO STAY ON THEIR FEET

246a THINGS FLYING INTO SHARKS MOUTH

246b QUINT SLIPPING ON DECK

246c OVER SHARK QUINT SLIDING INTO SHARKS MOUTH

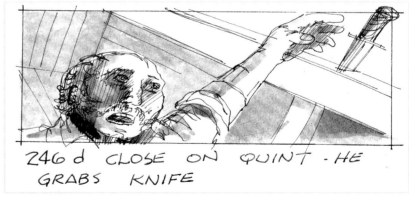

246d CLOSE ON QUINT - HE GRABS KNIFE

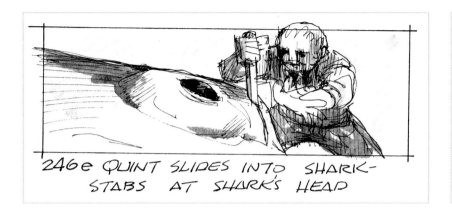

246e QUINT SLIDES INTO SHARK-
STABS AT SHARK'S HEAD

246f QUINT IN RAGE

246g SHARK GRABS QUINT

246h - SHARK TAKES QUINT

246A a BRODY SEES QUINT TAKEN
ORCA BOUNCES UP AND DOWN

246A b DOOR SLAMS SHUT, GIN POLE
FALLS TO BLOCK IT CLOSED

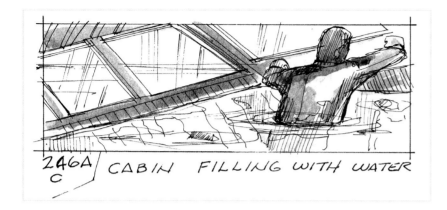

246A
c — CABIN FILLING WITH WATER

246A
d — BRODY HEADS FOR WINDOW

246A
e — BRODY REACTS WITH HORROR

246A
f — SHARK UNDERWATER COMING AT US

246A
g — SHARKS BREAKS THRU CABINS PORT WINDOW

246A
h — BRODY ON WINDOW LEDGE FINDS AIR TANK

246A i SHARK IN CABIN – BRODY SHOVES AIR TANK IN SHARKS MOUTH

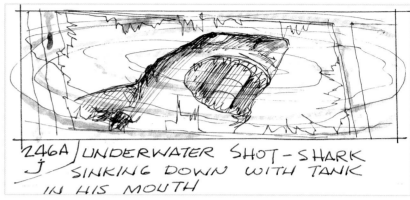

246A j UNDERWATER SHOT – SHARK SINKING DOWN WITH TANK IN HIS MOUTH

246A K BRODY'S HEAD IS CUT BY FLYING GLASS

246A L BRODY CLIMBS OUT OF WINDOW

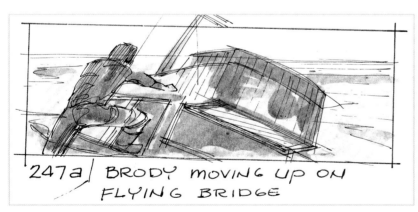

247a BRODY MOVING UP ON FLYING BRIDGE

247 b BRODY SLIDING ON WET DECK – SHARK SURFACES WITH TANK IN HIS MOUTH

247
c

BRODY GRABS GUN ON FLYING
BRIDGE

247
d

BRODY LOADING GUN MOVES
TO MAST

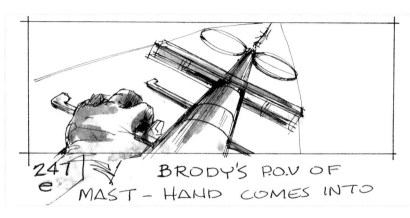

247
e

BRODY'S P.O.V OF
MAST - HAND COMES INTO

247
f

SHOOTING FROM MAST
BRODY CLIMBING UP

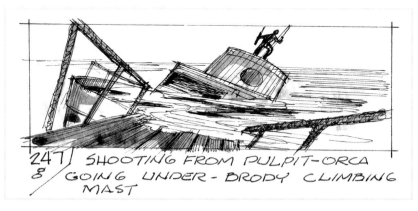

247
g

SHOOTING FROM PULPIT-ORCA
GOING UNDER - BRODY CLIMBING
MAST

248
a

BRODY'S P.O.V. - SHARK IN
WATER WITH TANK IN HIS MOUTH

248b / SHARKS P.O.V. BRODY SHOOTING

248 c / BRODY ON MAST SHOOTING AT SHARK

248 d / OVER BRODY SHOOTING AT SHARK

249   TANK-EXPLODES!

249A CLOSE ON BRODY - WATER, SHARK, ETC. EXPLODES

253 HOOPER COMES TO THE SURFACE - SEES BRODY IN THE BACKGROUND

253A HOOPER GRABS BARRELS—
TIES THEM TOGETHER

254 HOOPER WITH BARRELS
KICKS TOWARDS BRODY—BRODY

254A CLOSE ON BRODY—TURNS AND
SEE HOOPER—HOOPER HANDS
BRODY A LINE TO BARRELS

255 BRODY—HOOPER KICK
TOWARDS SHORE

FROM ART TO ACTION

WHEN THE CAMERAS ROLLED and the shark needed to bite, it was Joe Alves' teeth that were often clenched tight, watchful and sometimes worried over whether the terror he envisioned was translating properly to film. "We were all quite worried that the film would be technically faulty," producer Brown admitted, "that it wouldn't seem true." Alves and Spielberg, motivated by the technically woeful *Old Man and the Sea* all those months ago (had it only been months?), were determined to ensure their work wouldn't be held high as an example of how *not* to make a motion picture. Be they faithful or foolish, neither Alves nor Spielberg gave up on their original vision for the picture. But while the two men's grit was admirable, the producers still sought to hedge their bets and add assurance to their lofty hopes. Zanuck and Brown both asserted early on, "Real sharks – we need real sharks to sell this to audiences."

Alves heard the producers' demand but was quick to correct them: his interpretation of Benchley's tale wouldn't allow such a thing (one more time: real sharks can't be trained to perform). By his design, though, and through the realization of it by the Magnificent Seven (plus those added to the team), the not-real shark proved to be quite terrifying and, as it would turn out, convincing enough to frighten moviegoers.

"IT'S TRUE – at times it was difficult for us to believe that the shark would be taken seriously," Alves conceded, "and that audiences wouldn't just laugh at it. It made so much noise and was so hard to control during shooting. While we were filming, we never saw the footage properly cut together; we never got the full impact of the scenes. But Bob Mattey always believed in the shark, and I always believed in Bob Mattey. He just wouldn't give up on what he promised to me during our first meeting. He rallied his team, he rallied my team, he pulled us all together to make this work."

Despite a rough start and continual bemoaning that "the shark is not working" among the cast and crew, Mattey wouldn't relent. The sharks continued to flop and falter in the waters of Martha's Vineyard, adding true frustration and even professional peril to all involved, but both Mattey and Alves assured all onlookers that it would work.

And, as it went along, Alves became more involved in the effects and the various construction work than an art director typically would. Remember, it was an all-hands-on-deck situation and, as such, all did whatever was needed, whenever it was needed, wherever it was needed.

For a while, Alves was helping to test the full-sized tow shark. "I was working the controls from the effects barge to understand how it worked and

PREVIOUS SPREAD / Joe Alves and the Orca (left page). Local boatman Charlie Blair photographs a stunning moment as Bob Mattey declares, "Alright you SOBs… let me show you what my shark can do!" (right page).

how we could make it best perform for the camera, that is until Gary Woods approached me and said, 'You know, you're not in the effects union.' I said, 'Yeah, I know, but I'm concerned with how this will operate and how it will look.' 'Well, it's not really an art director's job; we should operate it.' 'Of course,' I said, and I stepped away from the controls, and I never had an opportunity to operate it again."

More unforgiving than union rules and regulations was the brutal ocean and the ambivalent weather patterns. And even when the waters were agreeable and the skies were clear, the mechanical shark remained complex, cumbersome, and challenging to control (remember, the filming pull up curtailed proper testing back in Southern California). So when the shark would misbehave, unexpectedly ramming into the *Orca* or having its exterior skin torn, the effects team – and often Alves himself – would make

the needed fixes to have the beast ready for its next take. But despite the efforts of the team, the sharks struggled to function in the salt water, even after a wholesale retrofitting to pneumatic operation when the sea's electrolysis rendered electronic operation useless. The team, then, struggled to get the redesigned sharks to work. Spielberg struggled to maintain his patience while awaiting them to function, shooting anything and everything else possible that wasn't the shark. And nobody – absolutely nobody – wanted those sharks to work more than Bob Mattey did. Despite the setbacks and the tremendous pressure he was under, including taking the brunt of the blame for those "great white turds," Mattey pressed on. He refused to give up. He all but forbade his team to give up, and he remained open to accepting additional insight and input from anyone who could assist in solving the team's shark problem.

ABOVE / The elaborate control deck that powers the shark.

LEFT / Joe Alves is waist deep and up to his elbows in the action.

The islanders, most notably the sometimes crass but absolutely indispensable seaman, Lynn Murphy, offered practical advice for refashioning the various shark apparatus for proper movement in the water. He didn't know a lick about fancy Hollywood effects but he did know about the water and especially how to navigate large craft – and maybe large mechanical creatures – through it. And Murphy wasn't a bit bashful to let these 'movie people' know when they had brought a pea shooter to a pistol fight. To the point, he looked at all the equipment needed to tow and operate the sharks then told the team they were woefully unequipped to tug it around.

"One evening, as the shooting of the land scenes was about to finish and we were faced with shooting the shark," Alves recalls, "I met with Zanuck and Brown. I'd had a couple of drinks in me and so I didn't mince words: I told them I thought we needed to be more aggressive in finding solutions and to spend money when money needed to be spent, and to bend and break rules when the production needed it to progress. They understood and agreed. Bill Gilmore also agreed, stepping in to take action on Lynn Murphy's advice. Next thing, we've secured for the effects team a capable barge, *The Whitefoot*, that could manage the operation of the various shark mechanisms. It made all the difference in the world, thanks to Lynn, Gilmore, and the agreeable producers."

LEFT / *The Whitefoot's* sturdy crane hefts the sea sled shark up and into the water for filming.

THIS PAGE / *The Whitefoot* positions the partially-sunk *Orca* alongside Spielberg and Alves in Zodiac raft (top). Left to right: Joe Alves, Richard Zanuck, Steven Spielberg, Bill Gilmore (right).

So partly on Murphy's advice and insight, aided by on-the-spot ingenuity of the effects team, the sharks began to rise, recede, and rampage on cue... mostly. Little by little, the specter of technical travails relented, gaining the company the kind of footage they needed to properly tell Benchley's tale. Their persistence was finally paying dividends, uneven though they may be, and editor Verna Fields was able to cut together some truly compelling sequences.

But there remained the nagging question: will audiences believe in the shark? The team agreed that it looked good despite all the noise it made, but

Alves and Gilmore still wanted an outsider's opinion regarding the realism of their great white wonder. To get that opinion, the experts would again need to be called in.

Alves believed the best folks to consult would be Australian shark experts, Ron and Valerie Taylor, who had already been involved in the *JAWS* production as a result of Zanuck's and Brown's previous insistence that the film contain footage of real sharks. That decree had been heeded and that suited Alves just fine: "One thing we can't film is the mechanical shark swimming away from the camera; all the hoses and

BELOW / Filming the death of the estuary boatman.

connections would be visible. Having footage of real sharks swimming away would solve that problem for us."

Alves tapped illustrator Tom Wright (with whom he had worked on television's *Night Gallery*) to render early storyboards of the underwater shark scenes, those that Spielberg had specified – scenes of the shark swimming in the open water as well as important shots of a real shark circling oceanographer Hooper's anti-shark cage. The Taylors were happy to comply, although Ron Taylor clarified: "Our sharks are usually only about fifteen or sixteen feet in length." Alves

and Spielberg agreed that they'd employ a little person, properly outfitted with small scuba gear and placed into a half-sized anti-shark cage, to give the needed up-sizing of the live sharks. The company dispatched Alves' former mentor, Frank Arrigo, to the area of Dangerous Reef in Australia where the Taylors would film the live sharks alongside a "little Hooper." And while Dangerous Reef lived up to its reputation (especially for the terrified Hooper stunt-double who narrowly escaped a real-life enactment of the oceanographer's scripted fate), the Taylors delivered the needed footage.

BELOW AND NEXT SPREAD / Illustrator Tom Wright's storyboards for the live-shark footage to be filmed by Ron and Valerie Taylor.

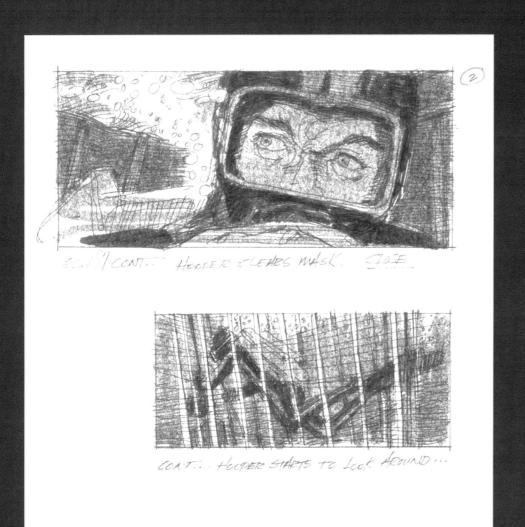

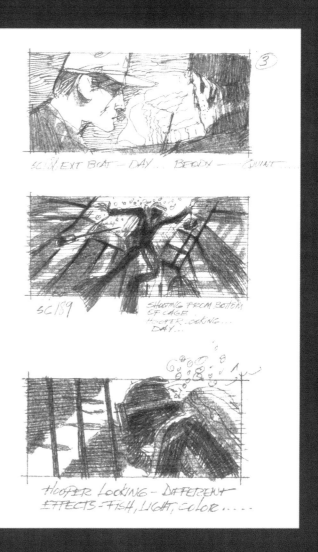

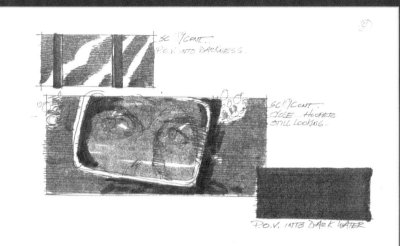

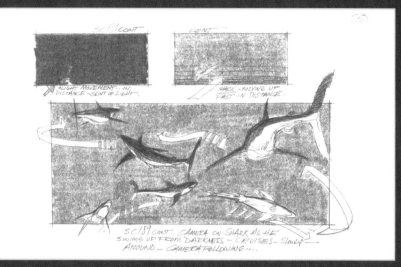

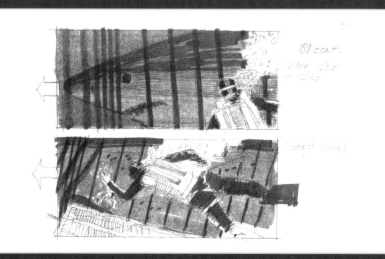

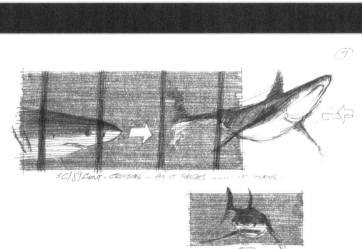

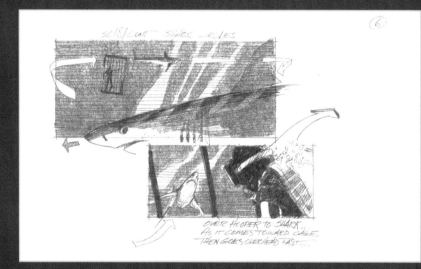

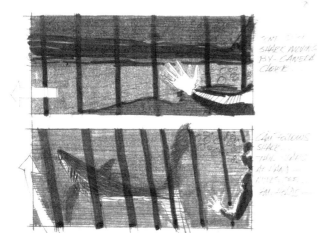

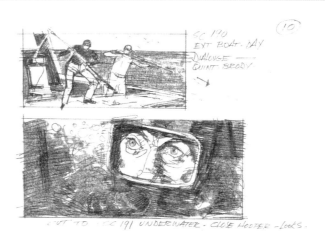

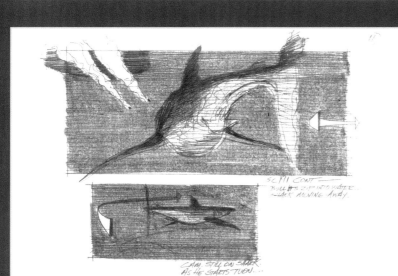

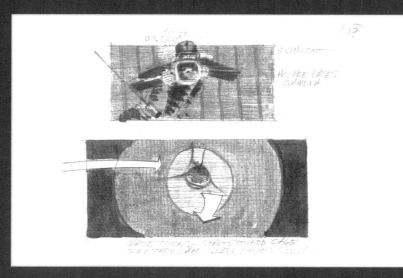

Now, many months later, the Taylors were asked to offer technical advice on the performance of the Magnificent Seven's mechanical marvel.

A screening of the shark footage was arranged and would include film editor Verna Fields. As Alves explains, "Verna needed to know what real sharks did and didn't do so she'd know how to cut the frames. She would be careful to not leave in anything that was inaccurate, especially in regards to the shark's look and its movements. It had to be as convincing as possible. Verna would also let us know, while she was editing as we were filming, what specific footage she might want or need in order to cut believable sequences."

On July 13, Fields ran rough-cut footage for the Taylors and their reaction brought sighs of relief: the sharks looked great! The Taylors praised the team for what they'd achieved.

The sharks, they said, moved very believably, remarkably so, even.

It was the validation everyone had been so hungry for, especially after having worried that the shark would look phony and elicit laughter. Not at all. If anything, Mattey and team had overshot the mark, giving the shark too much animation, so said the Taylors. And with that decree of approval from the experts, the production had finally crossed over from "it's impossible" to "it's incredible!" Not bad for a summer B-movie. The production pressed on as there were still many weeks to go, only now there was more confidence in the eventual outcome.

THIS SPREAD / The right-to-left shark in action (left). The transcript of Ron and Valerie Taylor's review of the shark performance (below).

CONVERSATION TAPED ON VIEWING OF FIRST FILM TESTS OF LEFT-TO-RIGHT PLATFORM SHARK

Joe Alves, Verna Fields, Ron Taylor and Valerie Taylor

July 13, 1974

VT: The only part that comes up is the eyes and perhaps part of the mouth.

JA: But they come up with a lunge, with a strong lunge - can they be clear of the gills out of the water?

RT: It can be, yeah, if they come out for food.

JA: But they can't come up in a vertical, can they?

VF: Like the shot you just saw there when he came up at an angle - what angle was that?

RT: He would then lunge; he would then fall back down.

VF: Do they come up with a force?

RT: Yes, yes, he would come up with a force and he would stay up there for a second or two; but then he would fall back.

VT: And he falls back quite quick.

VF: Does he fall down back?

RT: He falls forward, always forward, he never falls back down, he never slides back down.

JA: Well, that's a good thing to know. Now I want to ask about the eyes.

RT: The eyes will animate slightly, but mainly when they pass a large object, because they only move their eye to protect it from bumping into something, coming close to a boat or a cage; then he might move his eye. But out there, in the water, he doesn't, he doesn't flick his eye, he has no reason to.

VF: He flicks his eyes if he thinks there's food about, though?

RT: If there's food about, or if he's overexcited for some reason, he may flick it, but always when he's near a large, solid object where he might damage his eye.

VF: Well, in other words, when he's fighting the boat.

2.

CONTINUATION OF RON AND VALERIE TAYLOR TAPE

RT: And especially when he bites onto something, then he saws his head from side to side so that his teeth will cut. When he's sawing from side to side, he will nearly always have his eye rolled back, because it's then he might bump his eye and damage it.

VF: It's very good to know that, because all the third act stuff when he comes near the boat, the activity, he'll really work with the eyes there.

JA: Before he really gets into it, he could be less animated. When he gets a harpoon in him, I imagine he gets pretty upset there.

LAUGHTER

RT: Although it doesn't seem to worry him a great deal, because they seem to be a bit insensitive. They might swing, just for a moment, away from it, but they go back in. They go back to an orderly pattern of circling around. We haven't harpooned them, but we've given them some solid thumps and they've hurt themselves on propellors and sharp things on the boat, and it just doesn't worry them a great deal.

VT: But, darling, the harpoon is attached to a rope and, as soon as they feel the restriction, why, then they go mad.

RT: Then they fight against it. And when they get hooked by a big-game fisherman and they feel there's something restraining them, then they'll go crazy.

VT: We've had them a couple of times get tangled in the traces attaching our coach to the boat, and it gets them around the tail and they just go crazy. I remember when we were filming JAWS, you probably heard about it, a shark got caught.

VF: Yes, we have that film here - the rope goes around and around.

RT: A shark panics on an occasion like that.

JA: Can we go on? This keel line should probably be under water.

RT: Yes. You see, his tail is under the water. The only time his tail comes out of the water is when he makes a lunge through the water like that. Or, if he's bitten something and he's pulling it down, his tail mightsplash out of the water. Normally, his tail is under the water, the tip of it would be showing above water. No, that's

3

CONTINUATION OF RON AND VALERIE TAYLOR TAPE

okay, but he'd continue forward, he never stops, he's always moving forward.

JA: Is that right?

VF: In other words, he would not slide back that way?

VT: He could, he could fall back that way. He wouldn't do it deliberately.

RT: It could be, if he was going up that way and he saw something, he might come back.

VT: He'd relax..

RT: But normally swimming along he wouldn't. (More looking at film). That's not so bad. He doesn't go back though, he always goes down.

VT: I think you'd acheive a far more realistic effect if you really didn't bring the shark so far out of the water.

JA: Right.

VT: That's good, that's better.

RT: That's perfect, that's forward, that's how they do it, forward. That's great, that's perfect, that's terrific.

VF: Would you stop the machine and put a little piece of tape on there for me, Bill?

JA: The shark's come out and his head's just showing, we can just barely see the first gill.

RT: And his head is going from left to right.

JA: It's at about a 45 degree angle.

RT: Perhaps not waving quite so much.

VT: He's biting the water.

VF: As he goes?

VT: He's tasting it, they taste it.

JA: Great. And less side to side.

CONTINUATION OF RON AND VALERIE TAYLOR TAPE

RT: Not so much as that, a little. They're stabilized so well the head doesn't react so much.

JA: Okay. We didn't have the tail movements, so we were probably overtraining on there, what movement we had at that time.

VT: That distance out of the water was good.

RT: That was good. That's right. He comes out of the water like that.

VT: If he comes out of the water like that, he'd only stay there for a second. The mouth is too animated. They don't snuff around as quite as much as that.

JA: Oh, you mean they hold it open?

RT: Yes, they do tend to open and close it, but that was just a little bit exaggerated. I guess they're capable of doing it, but we just don't see them doing it.

JA: Would you say that when they're doing this, they're not really biting anything, they're just sort of grabbing at the water, that they would be moving slower?

RT: He's too far out of the water, far too far out.

JA: I think that's a good thing to remember, that he opens the mouth and closes it slower when he comes through the water, sometimes he just leaves it open as he travels through the water.

VT: He's tasting the oil or whatever it is on the surface, and he's following it with his mouth, with his taste buds.

RT: If we can go back again and have a look at that. If he was lungeing through the water, he'd do it quicker, he'd go up and then down.

JA: We had a malfunction with the tail. I think if the tail was wagging and he didn't come out of the water, it would be a little more realistic.

RT: He stays up too long, right, he stays up too long.

CONTINUATION OF RON AND VALERIE TAYLOR TAPE

JA: You see, we had an animated pectoral fin and it got too weak, so it kept coming up, so we've made it stiffer with very - with less movement.

RT: They don't move much, not so much, you don't notice any movement in the pectorals.

JA: We pretty much eliminated the movement because of that, because too much movement looked phoney. I didn't see much movement in your footage.

RT: No, it just hangs there.

JA: Good.

RT: They only use it to stop themselves in hurry. It's a brake.

JA: It's a turning-in effect.

VT: When they lunge, generally, as they go down, they give it a whack with their tail, I guess to pick up momentum. If you want to use the tail movement there, they sort of go Whack! Whack! as they go down. And the tail's always going as it swims.

RT: The head from side to side is not so much. No, the tail sweeps.

VF: When they're actually swimming like that you only see the tip of it?

RT: No, not that much, about there.

JA: Right at that break, that little indentation in the caudal fin.

RT: You'll see the dorsal and the tail like that sometimes.

VT: You've got to remember that he's a very heavy creature and that he can't do anything without the power in his tail. It's got to be able to lift him out and it's got to be able to hold him, so it's not very long.

JA: This is what we did for size relationship.

RT: Yes, but that's too much. You see he's foaming white water all around his eyes. There'll never be foam around his nose. Never. You see, the head is so streamlined that there's no foam around it.

6

CONTINUATION OF RON AND VALERIE TAYLOR TAPE

JA: We were simply overcompensating with the head to get some animation, but it's good to know. We cut down on that side to side. What do you think of the color right there?

RT: I think it's fairly good. They can be grayer, but they can't be any lighter.

JA: Okay, we can darken it a little. Again, you saw it when it was painted, because it wasn't nearly that light in the book. Well, I don't think we have any problem with the color now. (Sound of Kem).

RT: Just cut down on the movement of his head and have his tail sweeping more.

VT: They come up like that, but have him hold his head. He might move his head once but he never, not more than once - a hammerhead swings its head.

JA: That's the problem in describing the actions of this shark. People have seen other sharks, you know, where they zigzag through the water and they do various things.

RT: If he's trying to get at somebody, he might move his head from side to side. In a case like that, that's good, because sometimes when they bite the water, they will do that.

VT: Some of the smaller sharks do that, but they're not really swinging their heads, their whole bodies are going. He swims like a torpedo.

JA: A torpedo and his tail is propelling.

VT: There's sharks and there's sharks, do you agree?

JA: I'm not too fond of the snarl on this thing here. I think we can eliminate the snarl.

VF: Will he go down that way?

RT: Yes.

VF: Well, that will create a foam. As long as he doesn't create foam on his nose.

And then came August. It was time to film the full-bodied 'sea sled' shark for the scenes where Hooper, Brody, and Quint hunt and kill the beast in the open waters. The sea sled shark misbehaved as badly as its two half-brothers, again requiring all the ingenuity and insistence that Mattey and Lynn Murphy could throw at it. Alves looked on, keeping a close eye on the storyboards that were guiding the shooting while also ensuring that this shark he had first sketched practically a year ago was still looking like the monster he had imagined. Thankfully, it did and, soon, this one began to behave, too.

August then turned to September. Seeing that the open sea storyboards had been marked with their prominent red 'X's, Gilmore suggested the final confrontation scenes between the shark, Quint, and Brody be brought inland to the protection of Katama Bay. Brilliant! Consequently, it was also at this point that more of the sharks' malfunctions had been ironed out, leading Alves, Gilmore, and the effects team to lament how much better it all could have run if only they had been given an extra month or two back in California to fully test and perfect the mechanisms. Or maybe it wouldn't have mattered at all. It was a moot point now.

Hindsight aside, Alves was nonetheless relieved and reenergized to have reached this pinnacle in the production. "After the sharks had started working and we'd smoothed out enough of the technical problems to get some useful and convincing footage, we all became even more collaborative in coming up with ideas for new shots. In the final sequences, I suggested to Steven that the shark could crash through the *Orca's* cabin window as it was sinking. He agreed and so we storyboarded that and I asked Jimmy Woods to build three balsa-and-breakaway-glass mockups of that section of the cabin. We hung one of these off the dock at a spot where the water was deep enough to position and raise the shark to crash into it.

The first time the shark didn't move exactly how we wanted and it didn't look right even though it destroyed the first of the balsa mock-ups. One thing I did, though, was I had the effects guys tie bits of squid – provided by Jim Blair – to the shark's teeth. Steven asked me, 'What's all of that... that meat on his teeth?' I said, 'That's Quint! The shark just ate him and that's bits of him stuck in its teeth.' Steven laughed, thinking it was a nice touch and a fun idea."

LEFT / Bob Mattey and the 'sea sled' shark (top). Preparing to film the 'sea sled' shark (bottom).

RIGHT / The shark crashes into the *Orca* cabin, Take #3.

By mid-September, Spielberg had completed his shooting duties after capturing the scenes of Brody in his *mano a man-eater* confrontation and the explosive final destruction of the great white, that achieved with a dummy shark head that the effects team jam-packed with dynamite, cushioned by pounds of goopy squid. Spielberg got the shots in the more cooperative Katama Bay as suggested by Gilmore, then he departed for the mainland, leaving just a few pick-up shots that Alves would direct with the second unit.

"I had been interested in taking a hand at directing back when I was art director on *Night Gallery*. Some of the other crew on that show were getting opportunities to direct episodes and producer Jack Laird once said to me, 'You know, if you want to direct one, Joe, just let me know.' Unfortunately, I never got that opportunity on the show, but here was my chance to direct second unit on these pick-up shots.

"I needed to get the shots of the left-to-right shark coming out of the water as it took the Kintner boy. Steven had filmed the scenes of the boy actor but we needed the shot where the shark surfaces and bites into a dummy tied to the rubber raft. We shot this on September 18 – it would be the final shot on the location.

"It turned out to be really foggy that morning. I needed to have the shark platform set early for the scene but we couldn't see a thing for all the fog. The boat I was using to mark the platform's placement had an on-board radar, though. I wanted to set this thing precisely in the spot where the sun would be coming up in the morning, letting me get a naturally backlit view to sort of obscure the shark when it attacked the boy, but I only had the radar to guide me in setting up the platform. It was something I'd never done before but, when the fog lifted, I saw that the platform was in the exact spot where I wanted it.

"And so the action of the scene would have the shark rising from the water to bite the Kintner dummy secured to the raft while other kids in the foreground played in the water. I shot it several times but I wanted one specific shot where the rising sun would be exactly behind the shark. Just as I was ready to have the camera roll, Whitey Krumm dove into the water and started swimming to the raft. 'What are you doing? You're in the shot!' I hollered. He hollered back that the dummy was coming off the raft. 'No, no – it's OK,' I shouted, 'get out of the shot!' He finally did but I lost the position of the sun. I wanted that shot real bad.

"What I didn't want was any trouble with the DGA [Directors Guild of America] because they frowned upon anyone directing who wasn't a member of their union. After I directed this and a couple other minor shots, someone turned me in to the union. I got my wrist slapped for that."

No matter – the pickup shots were complete. The final task on the island was to work with the effects team and remaining crew to ensure the sharks were safely loaded back onto the trucks and returned to Los Angeles. On Saturday, the fleet of semis rumbled out of the Vineyard, taking the lights, the cameras, and all the action with them. Alves and the crew said their farewells. He, the crew, and the sharks were going home. But their work wasn't done yet.

The *JAWS* crew might have been out of the unforgiving ocean but they still weren't out of the water. Their next maritime task would be to film the sequence in which Hooper and Brody cruise the peaceful nighttime waters in search of the shark. In a welcome change from the angry Atlantic, the scene was shot at Falls Lake, the large pond on the Universal back lot that was once home to the *Sgt. Bilko* series. The crew laid down a thick blanket of fog, effectively adding an eerie mood to the scene though primarily done to obscure the fact that Hooper's boat wasn't actually skimming along the open ocean.

PREVIOUS SPREAD / Joe Alves sets the camera to film the shark attack on the Kintner dummy.

ABOVE / Vineyard resident, Carol Fligor, captures Super-8 footage of Joe Alves' filming of the Kintner attack.

RIGHT / Preparing the 'sea sled' shark in MGM's Esther Williams water tank.

Next was the underwater sequence where Hooper discovers the remains of fisherman, Ben Gardner, while swimming underneath the hull of the defunct vessel, the *Flicka*. And, of course, there would be the complex sequence where the shark would attack Hooper in his anti-shark cage. For both of these sequences, the crew set up in the Esther Williams tank at MGM Studios.

"We built a replica of the real cages that Ron and Valerie Taylor used in their diving," Alves explains. "We took the cage, the shark, and stuntman Richard Warlock to the tank at MGM. Since these shots didn't need a visible horizon line, we could get away with shooting them in a tank. The shark worked great – it did everything we wanted it to do, just the way we wanted to do it. It was Magnificent Seven team member, Whitey Krumm, who was operating it."

Alves also had a miniature of the shark built – the only miniature used in the picture – to capture the blown-up beast spiraling down into the blood-clouded water. That was also filmed in the MGM tank.

And, finally, it seemed the shooting was complete. The fate of the picture would be in the hands of editor Verna Fields, Spielberg at her side for the duration. When the two had a suitable 'work print,' (the music and sound effects still absent), it was time for John Williams to compose the picture's score while Carl Gottlieb reviewed the print with Spielberg and Fields to make any needed improvements or fixes in the dialog, those which could be looped by the actors after the fact.

It was in early March of 1975 when the first 'answer print' (with all final edits, music, sound effects, and fine-tuned dialog in place) was delivered to Universal. A special sneak preview screening was arranged in Dallas, Texas, scheduled to follow a showing of *The Towering Inferno*.

Spielberg was in attendance, nervous that the audience might laugh at the shark and, by extension, Hollywood might laugh at him. But the audience didn't laugh – they screamed. The picture captivated the crowd, who shared their enthusiasm for the film as they filled out their preview comment cards.

ABOVE / Joe Alves and Steven Spielberg float on the surface of the Esther Williams tank (top) while the shark attacks Hooper's cage below the surface (middle and bottom).

PREVIOUS PAGE / Joe Alves surveys the preparation of the 'sea sled' shark in the Esther Williams tank.

SPIELBERG WAS RELIEVED and yet this answer print wasn't the complete answer he was looking for.

"Steven called me up and explained that he wanted just a couple more shots," Alves remembers. "He wanted to show splintering planks and incoming water when the shark rammed the hull of the *Orca*. He also wanted to reshoot the sequence where Ben Gardner's head bobs out of the hole in the hull of the *Flicka*. From the test screenings, Steven thought he could get a better scream from the audience, much like the scream that came the first time the shark surfaces behind Chief Brody.

"I'd need to build sections of both hulls to do this and we'd need to gather a small crew to film it. Universal said there was no budget left and, therefore, there'd be no more shooting. Steven decided he'd pay for it himself. He really wanted these shots. We ultimately had to 'borrow' some of the camera and lighting equipment from Universal – even the prop of Ben Gardner's head – to get it done. Islander Kevin Pike, who worked with Ward Welton and the rest of us at Martha's Vineyard, was in California and doing some work for me around my home. I told him what we were going to do and he helped me build the two hull sections in my garage. Then, for the shot where the shark is ramming the *Orca* hull, we filmed that in my driveway one afternoon using a sledgehammer and some garden hoses to get the splintering of the planks and the water spray that erupts between them.

"For the reshoot of the Ben Gardner scene, we took that hull piece and the head to Verna Fields' pool. Steven dumped some milk into the water to get the proper opaqueness, then we filmed it with stuntman Frank Sparks doubling for Richard Dreyfuss. Kevin, from the interior side of the hull, pushed the head through the hole."

And Spielberg was right; the reshoot with the differently-timed appearance of the head got a better reaction – a bigger scream – during a second test screening at the Lakewood Theater in California. Alves attended this screening since he was just as concerned that the shark might elicit laughs. Again, it didn't – and this time it garnered applause.

THIS PAGE / Newspaper listing for the second test screening of *JAWS*.

Zanuck and Brown, along with Universal Studios executives Sid Sheinberg and Lew Wasserman, had also been at the screening and witnessed for themselves the remarkable audience reaction. They scurried to the theater restroom for an impromptu meeting. "We need to rethink the release plan for this picture," they excitedly agreed. "It's going to be a big hit!" And so it was – the first 'summer blockbuster.'

JAWS would ultimately gain Alves 'A-list' recognition among production designers. The film tested his skills, his creative instinct, and his professional and personal resolve. Despite its challenges and Universal's low expectations for it to be just another 'popcorn movie,' Alves and his team, along with director Spielberg and the rest, never gave less than their best effort.

"All the while, working on *JAWS*, none of us treated it as a low-budget picture," Alves asserts. "We gave it our best every day – everyone did – because we all knew we were only as good as what we produced."

And it was good, and it would be received and regarded as such around the globe. *JAWS* would become – and remain – a phenomenon.

❚❚ When many of the films on some 'ten best' lists are forgotten, *JAWS* will still be irresistible entertainment!"
GENE SHALIT, NBC-TV, 1975

THIS PAGE / Joe Alves and his team did what they said couldn't be done... and it was phenomenal...

JUST WHEN YOU THOUGHT IT WAS SAFE

DESPITE THE EXPLOSIVE FINALE OF *JAWS*, the persistent great white shark has proven itself to be exactly that – persistent. While audiences everywhere have cheered Chief Brody's on-screen triumph, they have alternately mourned the great white's demise. As Joe Alves has often noted, people just can't seem to get enough of this shark. Imagine, then, the thrill of discovering that one of the original sharks had survived! Well, sort of.

Although the original three filming sharks are long gone, a new wave of excitement swept the fandom upon rumors that another descendant still existed. Initially dismissed as myth and misrepresentation, those rumors of one more have now been proven to be fact – there was and is a fourth shark!

Universal requested a fiberglass copy of the shark to be displayed at the studio's popular theme park. This 'photo-op shark' thrilled visitors, who lined up to have their photographs taken alongside the tail-tied and vertically-hoisted replica. The shark remained a fixture within the tour's 'Prop Plaza' for over fifteen years, promoting *JAWS* and its three sequels.

But by 1990, park managers decided that the aging shark was in need of replacement. Universal routinely relocated its larger cast-offs, mainly stunt cars and now this weather-weary shark, so a call went out to Sam Adlen, owner of 'Aadlen Brothers Auto Wrecking' (aka 'U Pick Parts') in Sun Valley, California. Adlen purchased the shark and hoisted it up horizontally to hover high among the trees, as if to keep a watchful eye over the yard – not too *faah* from the *caahs*.

Over the years, Adlen received many generous offers to sell his 'junkyard shark,' all of which he refused. Those who felt jilted by the rejection cast aspersions, declaring the shark wasn't authentic, that it was just a spurious creation of unknown origin. But was it? This would become a topic of debate for years to come – twenty years, to be exact.

In 2010, NPR journalist and *JAWS* enthusiast Cory Turner called in two experts who could settle the matter: Joe Alves and Roy Arbogast. With the approval of Adlen's son Nathan (Sam having passed away in 1998), Alves and Arbogast carefully examined the shark with forensic deliberateness. Atop a ladder, Arbogast studied the replica more closely, noting details of the visible seam lines and recognizable contours from the mold he had made over forty years ago. After a few minutes, he concluded that, yes, indeed, this shark had been fashioned from his original mold. A fourth shark! Proudly, Adlen insisted that it remain in his yard: that's what Dad would have wanted.

RIGHT / Joe Alves, Roy Arbogast, and the 'junkyard shark.'

In 2016, Adlen closed U Pick Parts and saw to the disposition of all its contents, including the shark. In an applause-worthy gesture, Adlen refused all offers for the shark and instead donated it to the new Academy Museum of Motion Pictures. Gratefully accepting the gift, the museum's team arranged for the shark to be relocated to an undisclosed site while they sought to identify the best person to restore this important – and authentic – artifact. It was Joe Alves who immediately suggested Greg Nicotero, the acclaimed special effects wizard and director of *The Walking Dead* (just one achievement from his impressive list of film and television credits that's longer than the twenty-five-foot shark). "No one else knows the shark as well as Greg," urged Alves. "With him, I believe the original design is in the most capable hands."

For Nicotero, *JAWS* will forever be the pivotal film that compelled him to pursue filmmaking – not only effects but also design, direction, and production oversight – and the one he will continue to study in his unending quest for additional

BELOW / April 2019: The fiberglass shark exterior is sanded, repaired, and primed (top left) while Joe Alves and Greg Nicotero discuss details of the new mouth (top right). Greg Nicotero and Dennis L. Prince (bottom left) and the magnificent new team (bottom right) includes, from left, Kevin Pike, Eddie Zarate (kneeling), Greg Nicotero, Joe Alves, Roger Baena, and Scotty Fields.

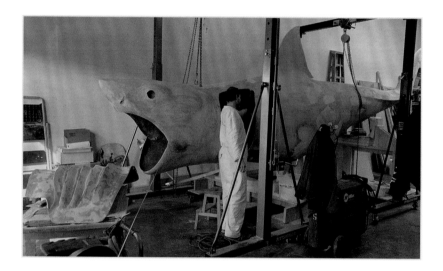

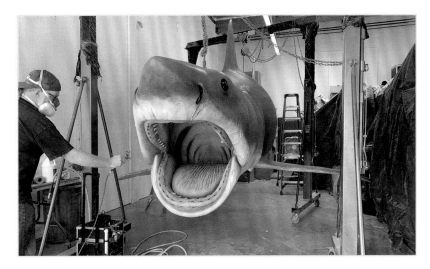

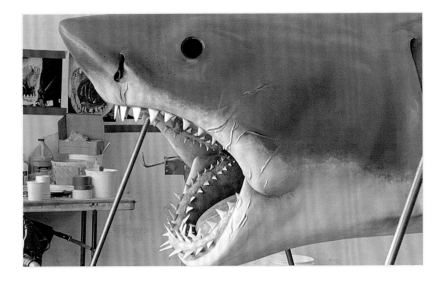

information, enlightenment, and inspiration. "What's most interesting about this fiberglass shark," Nicotero revealed, "is that it's the most accurate representation of the original sculpture; the flexible skin [taken from Roy Arbogast's mold] was slid over the internal operating mechanisms and, because of that, it would stretch and distort a bit, but this rigid fiberglass replica didn't allow for any distortion. It's the most authentic version of the original design and, for me, it's been fascinating to be able to examine it in this way." And with the new revelations

this junkyard shark now provides, Nicotero continues to discover new details about the great white shark he has long revered that add to the achievements of the technicians he has admired for decades.

As for Joe Alves, he continues to be amazed that people of all walks and from everywhere in the world still talk about *JAWS* with such passion. The shark's restoration, commissioned by the Academy Museum, is a fitting tribute to everyone involved in the making of the film. It will surely inspire new generations of moviegoers and moviemakers.

ABOVE / Greg Nicotero attends to the new mouth detail (top left). Craig Fraser gives the shark an accurate paint finish, inside and out (top right). The restored and refinished shark is nearly ready to claim its territory in the Academy Museum (bottom left and right).

AFTERWORD
BY JOE ALVES

WHEN YOU WORK IN THE FILM INDUSTRY for so long, as I did, and you find yourself moving up in positions – like starting as a junior set designer and hoping to someday become an art director – you always look forward to work, to the next job. Through the 'studio system' of the time, you were generally assigned work by the head of the art department and I worked hard to advance up the ladder. Along the way, I was fortunate enough to work directly with some really influential people like Alfred Hitchcock, even though I was still just making my way up the ladder. I got my own shows, though, when I worked in television: that is, shows where I was assigned as art director. That was great because it would become my step to hopefully get a feature film to work in that capacity; you were always looking up and looking ahead in this business. And so it was a big break for me to become the art director for *Rod Serling's Night Gallery* and a bunch of made-for-TV movies because that ultimately led to *The Sugarland Express*, my first feature as art director and my first feature work with Steven Spielberg.

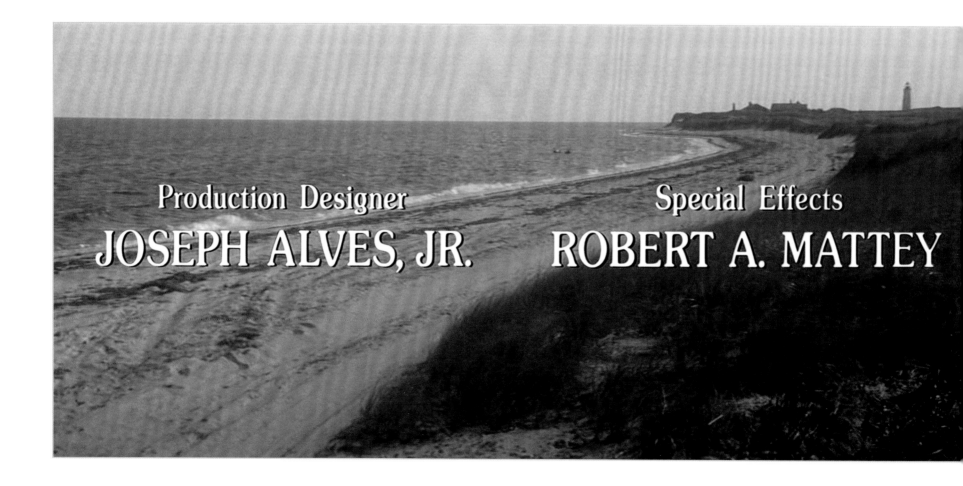

Production Designer
JOSEPH ALVES, JR.

Special Effects
ROBERT A. MATTEY

And then came *JAWS*.

When I did *JAWS*, it came as a big challenge. The fact that Marshall Green gave me the total autonomy to go out and find a crew to make the shark, and to take it off the lot, gave me a tremendous amount of power not normally afforded to an art director at that time – and only a very few people were regarded as production designers back then. And so this made *JAWS* a big deal in my career, for the freedom that was afforded to me and, by the time we would finish, that my credit would be changed to "Production Designer."

But there was a lot of trouble with the shark and the filming, and when we came back to Universal from Martha's Vineyard, we weren't heroes. We were way over budget, way over schedule, and we still had more to do. At that moment, there wasn't a lot of respect for what we had achieved. The shark was put out onto the studio back lot, basically to rot, one of the *Orcas* was sold off, and there just wasn't much regard for what we had done. And then the film was released and it was a big financial success – I think it made back its budget in the first week. It was gratifying to everyone who had worked so hard – and everyone did – and the reaction to it was amazing. But, then, that was that.

JAWS, then, was a job that was done; it was in the past – that was my thinking at the time. I needed to move on to my next work, Steven would move on to his next work; we all would. It's what you do after you complete a picture, so I went on to do a small picture called *Embryo* and I think Steven was considering doing something else. As it soon turned out, Steven and I were able to work together again on *Close Encounters of the Third Kind*, and that was a big success. Of course, I also went on to work on

JAWS 2 and to direct *JAWS 3-D*.

But what has surprised me most about *JAWS* is how it came back to be a really big deal at the start of this new century, and it continues to be. There were the big JAWSFest events at Martha's Vineyard, and I've attended many of these special shows and events with other *JAWS* cast and crew – MonsterPalooza, WonderFest, SharkCon, The Hollywood Show, and so many more – and the people just can't seem to get enough of it. They love *JAWS*.

To this day, I get requests for copies of my artwork and my signature every week from all around the world. *JAWS* is really important to a lot of people and, for what we all achieved in doing the picture, I'm glad to see folks enjoying it so much, now more than forty years since it was released.

JAWS just won't go away, and I'm thankful for everyone out there who keeps it alive.

Joe Alves

ACKNOWLEDGMENTS

WHILE IT WAS SO REWARDING to see my "Production Designer" credit for *JAWS*, it was largely thanks to the incredibly committed people with whom I worked. My thanks to set decorator John Dwyer, painter Ward Welton, and carpenter Jimmy Woods. Thanks, also, to the local Vineyard folks we hired on who helped us achieve our goals.

We were fortunate to have such highly-supportive producers, Richard D. Zanuck and David Brown, who always urged that we keep going.

Bill Gilmore was the perfect production executive for the picture and with whom I had worked quite well before and after *JAWS*.

Of course, the 'Magnificent Seven' included Roy Arbogast, Ritchie Helmer, Tim Baar, Gary Wood, Mike Wood, Conrad 'Whitey' Krumm, and Stan Mahoney. Also, sculptor Don Chandler and draftsman, Frank Wurmser.

Vineyard boat wrangler Lynn Murphy and wife Susan were of tremendous help, showing us all we needed to know about towing mechanical sharks through the island waters.

I especially want to thank Steven Spielberg, a director with whom I developed a great working relationship. I'm very proud of what we accomplished on *JAWS* and I'm glad that we held fast to our original vision.

Finally, I offer my dedication of this book to the leader of the Magnificent Seven, Bob Mattey. If there was a 'spirit' of the production, it came via Bob's never-ending positivity.

It was truly an honor in my career to have worked with everyone who made *JAWS* such an enduring picture.

Thank you, everyone.

– JOE ALVES, JUNE 2019

WRITING A BOOK ABOUT *JAWS* has been an absolute joy and honor for me. I never could have expected this opportunity back when I was just a twelve-year-old kid.

Over the course of this adventure, I've had the remarkable good fortune to befriend Joe Alves. He's been a tremendous inspiration to me, personally and professionally. Thank you, Joe, for your unwavering support.

The *JAWS* enthusiasts are a wonderful bunch! Thanks to Jim Beller (JAWSCollector.com) for providing additional photos, information, and connections to others in this community.

Vineyard author Matt Taylor has been an equally indispensable resource for fleshing out key details.

Always-generous Chris Kiszka shared his amazing collection of film props and wardrobe from *JAWS*.

Clint Schultz provided top-notch image scanning and preparation. Also, Jerri Lauridsen and Jan Lauridsen provided early copy review.

Sincere thanks for additional content and permissions from Jeff Pirtle and team at NBC/Universal and Kristin Stark at Amblin Partners.

Thanks to Greg Nicotero for the wonderful foreword plus access to the 'junkyard shark' restoration (with kind permission from Denise Bratton, Sophie Hunter, and others at the Academy Museum of Motion Pictures).

Additional thanks to everyone who shared their personal photos seen in this book: Cal Acord, Charlie Blair, Edith Blake, Andy Caulfield, Carol Fligor, Ritchie Helmer, Douglas Kennedy (JAWSFinatics), Wayne Lacono, Susan Murphy, Rita Orr-Schmidt, Cory Turner, Dick Whitney, and Al Wilde.

Of course, thanks to Ellie Stores, Natasha MacKenzie, Simon Ward, and the team at Titan Books.

Thank you, all, for making this such an exciting experience.

– DENNIS L. PRINCE, JUNE 2019